REDISCOVERING PRAYER

Communicating with ALLAH

BASSAM SAEH

Translated from the Arabic by
Nancy Roberts

THE ISLAMIC FOUNDATION

A revised, abridged version of the Arabic original,
Prayer Management
Communicating with Allah: Rediscovering Prayer

Published by
THE ISLAMIC FOUNDATION,
Markfield Conference Centre, Ratby Lane, Markfield,
Leicestershire, LE67 9SY, United Kingdom
E-mail: publications@islamic-foundation.com
Website: www.islamic-foundation.com

Quran House, Po Box 30611, Nairobi, Kenya

PMB 3193, Kano, Nigeria

Distributed by
KUBE PUBLISHING LTD
Tel: +44(0)1530 249230, Fax: +44(0)1530 249656
E-mail: info@kubepublishing.com

4th impression,2024

British Library Cataloguing in Publication Data

ISBN: 978-0-86037-715-3 Paperback
ISBN: 978-0-86037-720-7 Ebook

Translated and edited by Nancy Roberts
Cover design and Typeset by Nasir Cadir
Printed in Turkey by Elma Basim

In the Name of Allah the Most Beneficent and the Most Merciful

This book has been written for the sole purpose of pleasing God Almighty.

Hence, the author requests everyone who reads this book to be generous with his or her comments, ideas, opinions and corrections so that future printings, in whatever language they appear, will be richer, more correct and more complete than the present one. To this end, readers are urged to write to the author at bassamsaeh@hotmail.com. When alterations or additions are made to the book, they will be attributed to those who proposed them so that they can enjoy a share in this ongoing gift to others.

Contents

Supplication VII

1. An Appointment with God 1
2. 'And this, indeed, is a hard act...': But Why? 8
3. From Duty to Privilege 10
4. The Satisfaction of Waking up Early for Prayer 15
5. The Joy of Patient Perseverance 19
6. Why Do we Pray? 25
7. The Rhythm of Prayer and the Rhythm of Life 34
8. Variety: The First Lesson in Civilisation 37
9. The Call to Prayer and its Ten Wonders 45
10. The Two Ritual Ablutions 54
11. Communal Prayer: The Key to Advancement and Civilisation 60
12. The Friday *Khuṭbah* (Sermon): A Course in Development 70
13. The Five Lines of Prayer 81
14. Red Key No. 1: 'God is Greater' 89
15. Reading, Reciting and Chanting 92
16. The New Language of the Qur'an 95

17. Open Language and 'Fertile Spaces' 98
18. The Role of the *Fātiḥah* 102
19. Red Key No. 2: 'You alone do we worship, and unto You alone do we turn for aid' 112
20. The Centrality of Bowing and Prostration 122
21. Red Key No. 3: 'Blessed Greeting to God' 127
22. Red Key No. 4: 'Peace be upon us...' 131
23. A Session for Supplication and Private Worship 134
24. Computing Profits and Losses 137
25. Let Your Whole Life be a Prayer 146

Endnotes 154
Index 158

SUPPLICATION

O God, You know that in recording the thoughts that appear on these pages, all I have sought is Your face, and Your good pleasure in the hereafter. If I have sought You in the words of my limited, feeble human language, it is because, ordinary human being that I am, addressing ordinary human beings, these words are all I have, inadequate though they are to reflect Your glory or to contain Your majesty and greatness. Hence, should my steed stumble on the way, sending me tumbling to the ground, it was, at least, on my way to You that I fell. And if I have erred or my tongue slipped, You know well that from start to finish, my only desire has been to attain to the truth of what You Yourself desire. How can we mortal humans fathom the depths of Your wise purposes, or the mysteries You revealed to Your Prophet in his nocturnal ascent as he received Your Divine instructions to institute our five daily prayers, whose precious treasures and secrets he then shared with us on Earth?

O God, if I have hit the mark, then reward me with the best with which You reward Your righteous servants. And if, in my thinking, appraisal, interpretation or expression, I have missed the mark such that, in my zeal to convey Your majesty, I have spoken in haste or my pen has led me astray from the path of Your wisdom, then reward me based on what You know, glory be to You, of my desire to be illumined by Your guidance alone, and to drink from the springs of Your compassion for all. You are, and will ever remain, the Most-Forgiving, the Most-Pardoning, the Most Loving and Generous One, the Most Merciful of the merciful.

From one who ever seeks refuge in Your grace

Bassam Saeh
Fajr, Friday, 15 Jumādā al-Ulā, 1436 AH
6 March, 2015 CE

1

An Appointment with God

'Prayer management?!' he asked in astonishment. 'Is prayer something one "manages"?' I responded, 'Take the case of people who study business management and finance. They do so in order to make the best material investments, to realise the highest rates of return, despite profits being temporary lasting for the duration of their life only. So, why shouldn't we manage our spiritual affairs in the same vein, that is make the best investments in this life to reap the greatest profits in the hereafter, especially when we know the rewards of the hereafter to be eternal, and never depleted? Could there be anything worthier of a person's investment and proper management than a singular activity like Salah (canonical prayer) that is intended to serve the good of both this world and the next?'

One day during the month of Ramadan the Saudi Students' Club at Oxford invited me to give a lecture right before the breaking of the fast. I accepted and decided to speak on the topic of 'Salah management'. At the scheduled time I went up to the pulpit. In my hand was a piece of paper on which I had jotted down two verses from the Qur'an and two sayings of the Prophet (pbuh) on Salah. After delivering the accustomed greeting, I unfolded the piece of paper and hurriedly read its contents, so fast in fact that the audience could hardly understand a word I had said. Within one minute I had finished and was heading for the door. On my way out I blurted, 'Pardon the rush, but I have an appointment to keep with people a lot more important than you are. Goodbye!' As I made a beeline for the door, I glanced out of the corner of my eye and noticed the faces of my tongue-tied listeners registering a mixture of protest, bewilderment, disbelief, and just possibly, offence and disapproval.

An understandable spontaneous human reaction given my impolite conduct towards people I had agreed to meet with. So, taking this a step further, what do we suppose the reaction would be if I conducted myself in the same manner towards God?

A few seconds later I returned and apologised to the students for my behavior, saying, 'Are you angry with me? Well, I have acted this way towards you once, and now I have come back to apologise. But the fact is, we act this way towards God an average of five times a day, yet without a single pang of conscience, and without a single word of apology!'

What a great opportunity, what a sweet rendezvous we miss out on when we scrimp on the time we give to God and offer our prayer in the same hurried manner with which I addressed the students – if, that is, it deserves to be called 'prayer' at all.

You will also notice that rather than reciting the Qur'anic verses and sayings of the Prophet to the audience from memory, I simply read them out from a piece of paper. But which would have had more impact on the listeners – reading from a piece of paper, or speaking contemporaneously? Ordinarily we perform Salah in the same way, that is, as if we are reading from a piece of paper, and as such, the words come out of our mouths, and not out of our hearts.

The Almighty has presented us with a tremendous gift, a vast investment project served on a platter of gold, yet we spurn it in contempt. As a result, we end up with nothing but what we might reasonably expect, namely, rejection and possibly even chastisement, for responding to God's gift with such ingratitude.

We need to realise within us the value of this gift and teach it to our children. That is, if we want our children to go beyond memorisation and imitation and join the ranks of true thinkers and innovators, we need to rediscover both ourselves and our forms of worship. Then we need to teach our children a way of thinking that will help them to rediscover everything around them, including the array of awe-inspiring inventions at their disposal.

I remember once in the late 1940's, as a child of seven or eight years old, my mother coming home from a visit to a Christian family in Lattakia telling us of an amazing 'radio' that their son had brought back from France on completion of his studies there. This 'radio' she informed us had a window in the front through which you could see the person who was speaking! I could not sleep that night for excitement, my child's imagination thinking of the poor radio announcer who I envisaged stuffed into the little box. How had they managed to get him inside it? They must have had to find somebody with a body tiny enough to fit. But then, my child's mind wondered, how would he be able to get out to go to the bathroom? Scores of questions of this sort hounded me all that night. Years later, I realised of course the device my mother had been talking about was a television!

Our children are being born into a world filled with televisions, radios, smartphones, computers, iPads (tablets), CDs, satellites, aeroplanes, cars, and other remarkable devices. As a consequence, they rarely think about how great these inventions really are. Nor do they give any thought to the greatness of the individuals who invented and developed them, or the thrill that must have accompanied their first introduction into people's lives. We need to train our children to be aware of the greatness of these things, since this will help them rediscover the greatness of creation, both within themselves and around them, and the greatness of God in the act of creation. This in turn will lead them to rediscover their religion and its forms of worship. Rather than leaving them buried beneath a stultifying layer of familiarity, habit, and repetition, they can learn to appreciate them anew as though they were becoming acquainted with them for the first time. Many verses of the Qur'an likewise train us in the art of rediscovery:

> [Hallowed be] He who has created seven heavens in full harmony with one another: no fault will you see in the creation of the Most Gracious. And turn your vision [upon it] once more: can you see any flaw? Yea, turn your vision [upon it] again and yet again: [and every time] your vision will fall back upon you, dazzled and truly defeated.... (*al-Mulk* 67:3-4)

> Have they, then, never beheld the birds above them, spreading their wings and drawing them in? None but

> the Most Gracious upholds them: for, verily, He keeps all things in His sight. (*al-Mulk* 67:19)

> Say [unto those who deny the truth]: 'What do you think? If of a sudden all your water were to vanish underground, who [but God] could provide you with water from [new] unsullied springs?' (*al-Mulk* 67:30)

People raised with an attitude of awe and wonder inspired by the Qur'anic approach to the world, will find themselves in a never-ending state of 'rediscovery', both of themselves and their surroundings. As a consequence, they and their society will enjoy a continuing state of cultural and spiritual growth and development. Every morning we are called upon to look at ourselves and the world around us through new eyes as though seeing them for the first time. Once we do so, we will see how much closer we are to God.

Our schools, institutes and university departments have seen the rapid spread of disciplines and curricula that concern themselves with the study of the best means of managing industrial, commercial, agricultural and construction projects, and of investing everything that has the potential of achieving profit and benefit in our lives both public and private. But who has ever thought of introducing a discipline or course of study that deals with the management and investment of something more valuable, more beneficial, more enduring, and more guaranteed to yield results both in this world and the next than all the aforementioned enterprises combined, namely, our various forms of worship, and first and foremost, Salah, which is, in essence, an appointment with God? In fact, such a field of study would contribute to the success of our transient worldly enterprises.

Salah is an encounter that occupies first place among the various forms of Islamic worship, which might be thought of as worldly-otherworldly investments. Hence, it should come as no surprise to learn that Salah (to perform prayers during their specified time periods) takes first place, ahead of the command to honour one's parents even:

> ʿAbd Allāh Ibn Masʿūd said: 'I once asked the Messenger of God (pbuh), "Which, of all actions, is the most pleasing to God?" And he said, "Performance of the prayers at their specified times". "Then what?" I asked. "Honouring one's parents." "Then what?" I asked. "Engaging in struggle (jihad) on God's behalf".'[1]

This is a remarkable Hadith, although most of us pass over it without much thought. Looking closely, the classification of placing Salah before honouring one's parents and jihad not only illustrates the great value of Salah, but also points to the importance of our loyalty to, and relationship with, parents, societies and in fact the entire world. We are to honour the world and make it a better place through struggle (jihad) for justice and human rights. Although the term's ethos is a noble one, tragically in our time it has been widely abused and misrepresented, hijacked and falsified by political and religious groups to justify their savage acts of terrorism and murder, when the Prophet of Islam was sent only as a mercy to all the world. For Salah to surpass by far even jihad in importance, virtue and reward is something that truly calls for reflection. It is even described by God Almighty as 'a hard thing' (*kabīrah*) for all but those who are 'humble in spirit' (*al-khāshiʿūn*). For such individuals, Salah poses no burden or difficulty because, by virtue of their humble reverence, they find it to be a source of enjoyment, tranquility and peace of mind, as well as a bulwark of protection in their lives. In fact, given a commitment to humble reverence and to deliberateness and patience in one's recitations, movements, reflection and imagination, prayer serves as a spiritual school that trains the believer in patient endurance, mental concentration, attention, modesty, acceptance of others and the ability to listen to them, calm nerves, careful, deliberate decision-making, moderation in one's attitudes, avoidance of impetuous, hasty or extreme judgments, and wisdom in dealing with other people and life situations. Hence, it should come as no surprise that in more than one passage of the Qur'an, God Almighty links prayer with patience and endurance:

> And seek aid in steadfast patience and prayer: and this, indeed, is a hard thing for all but the humble in spirit. (*al-Baqarah* 2:45)

> And bid your people to pray, and persevere therein. (*Ṭa Ha* 20:132)

2

'And this, indeed, is a hard act...': But Why?

Why pray?

Why should we cancel our appointments, put aside the work we are doing, interrupt our business, and put everything else in our daily lives on hold, no matter how important it happens to be, in order to turn to prayer? Why did the Messenger of God identify prayer as the factor that distinguishes a believer from an unbeliever? Why was it prayer in particular that the Prophet reminded his community of, from upon his deathbed, saying, 'For the sake of God, do not abandon prayer!'

Was prayer originally established in Muslims' lives as a punishment, or as a reward? What aspects of it are difficult, and what aspects of it enjoyable, if we do, in fact, find any enjoyment in it? Why are we instructed to pray at these particular times, with these particular movements, and this particular number of bows and prostrations? Why are we to utter these particular words and do these particular recitations? Why is prayer found in all religions? How is it that God and His Messenger place even greater importance on prayer than they do on jihad?

I have to confess that I had been praying for a full fifty years before I discovered that in prayer, God Almighty had bestowed on me the greatest commercial enterprise anyone could hope to possess, and that if I chose wisely how to manage and run this enterprise, I would stand to reap the richest harvest and experience the fullest enjoyment anyone on Earth could dream of.

Suppose you happen to witness a battle between two groups of ants over a tiny lump of sugar: One ant pounces on its opponent's back, another digs its little claws into its enemy's leg to prevent it from getting to the lump of sugar, and still another charges at this or that member of the enemy camp. You will probably stand there chuckling at this peculiar battle between the two little armies. And over what? Over a tiny piece of sugar that, in human terms, would be considered of no value at all.

Now suppose you performed a truly perfect prayer, one that left you feeling as though you had been lifted out of the earthly realm and straight to the throne of God. If you then looked down on the world from those lofty heights, you would see everything in it, no matter what its size, as so minute as to be hardly visible with the naked eye. You would see that the miserable piece of sugar that the ants have been warring over is none other than our trifling life on Earth, and that the foolish little ants in mortal combat over a piece of sugar represent you and whatever group or groups of people you are at odds with over that piece of sugar.

3

From Duty to Privilege

Indeed, Salah in our Islamic tradition may start out as a duty. As the Prophet is reported to have said that children are to be positively encouraged to pray when they are ten years old.[2] Similarly, the Prophet stated, 'Nothing stands between a man and unbelief but the neglect of Salah.'[3] Ideally, however, when children reach the age of discernment and comprehend the nature and dynamics of Salah, they will discover the importance of this hotline to God for themselves, and the concept of 'duty' will gradually be replaced by that of 'privilege' or 'right'.

When our children are young, we have to force them to take their medicine. But as they mature, they go from seeing medicine as an affliction to be endured to seeing it as a right to be enjoyed or appreciated, since they realise that medicines can restore them to health and even save their lives.

Imagine that you are about to sign a lease on a large house. You are enchanted by its beauty, its spaciousness, its lovely location and its elegant furnishings. But when you sit down to negotiate the rent with the landlord, he surprises you by saying, 'In lieu of the rent, I require you to eat five delectable meals a day at my expense. That's what I require – no more, no less.'

What an offer that would be! And in fact, it's the very offer we have received from God Almighty in return for our living on this Earth of His, enjoying its bountiful blessings and helping to populate it and build it up. This being the case, don't we wrong ourselves by not giving our daily prayer 'meals' the time and attention we devote to the meals we take into our bodies? Why do we begrudge our spiritual nourishment the time we give so freely of to our physical nourishment? Which of them do you suppose is more important for us?

Have you ever heard of a major prize whose donor stipulates that before receiving it, the winner must first accept another major prize? What kind of a prize might that be? The prize I am referring to is Salah. We will not receive our great reward from God unless we first collect the wonderful spiritual prize He has given us by enjoying its performance as a right and privilege rather than merely enduring it as a duty or burden.

'If a servant of God rises to pray, all his sins are brought and placed on his shoulders, and as he bows or prostrates, they fall away.'[4] Similarly, 'Any Muslim who performs a thorough ablution, then sets out to pray, being aware of what he is saying, will revert to being as pure as he was on the day he was born.'[5] So as you begin your prayer with the words, 'God is greater!' (*Allāhu Akbar*!) imagine the angels bringing all the sins you have ever been guilty of and piling them on your shoulders so that as you bow or prostrate, they come tumbling off.

How easily a right can come to feel like a duty, possibly even a burdensome one that we want to be freed from as quickly as possible. This is the experience of those who feel as though they are 'losing' or 'wasting' the precious time they spend performing a few cycles of prayer. Duty is something we invariably associate in our minds with a burden, something that weighs on us. As such, we see it as something that impoverishes us rather than enriches us, since it deprives us of time or rest we see ourselves as being entitled to. With this perception a distortion begins, and for many people, prayer begins to be transmuted into a burden that they are anxious to be relieved of. Quite to the

contrary, however, the Messenger of God portrayed prayer as something that brings rest and relief. Did he not say, 'Give us repose through [prayer], O Bilāl!'?[6]

So, rather than asking ourselves, 'Have I prayed?', however critical this question might be, let us instead ask, 'When I prayed, did I receive the prize that had been designated for me? Did I truly enjoy it as I pondered the earthly blessings it brings me, and did I savor the thought of the riches I am saving up for the life to come?'

Let your prayer be a free ticket to a pleasant journey, not simply around the world, but around the universe, one in which you gain access to the King and Absolute Ruler of the cosmos.

Duties vs. Rights

Duties in our lives are often confused with rights to the point where we don't know where one ends and the other begins. For example, the Hajj, or pilgrimage to Makkah, is a duty that requires determination, travel, expenditure of energy and monetary outlay. It may even involve some danger and risk.

But when we think about the reward that awaits us for every step we take along the way, the sense of duty will begin to evaporate and be replaced by an awareness of the pilgrimage as a right and a privilege.

Similarly, the giving of charity is a duty that involves effort and expense. But when we undertake it with willing hearts, and with a realisation of the reward we can anticipate along with the happiness we have given to the people we have helped, we will be showered with peace and tranquility for having pleased our Lord and for the protection, warmth and safety we made possible for someone in need.

Fasting, too, is a duty, an obligation that requires us to endure hunger and thirst and to exercise patience and self-control. But with every minute that passes, we anticipate the enjoyment of God's promised reward and the pleasure of drawing near to God as we obey His commands and heed His prohibitions. The reward is not limited simply to the fast-breaking meal that follows a long day of hunger and thirst. Rather, it includes the satisfaction of having triumphed in a battle with our egos' cravings and added to our lasting store of Divine approval.

The same principle applies to the Islamic categories of permissible (*ḥalāl*) and forbidden (*ḥarām*). God Almighty only forbids things to us in order to protect us from some harm, whether or not we realise the nature of the harm involved. Similarly, when God declares something permissible to us or commands us to perform a given action, it is for the sake of some benefit. Hence, we might speak of *ḥalāl* and *ḥarām* as 'beneficial' and 'harmful' respectively, whether in the realm of economics, psychology, medicine or whatever else.

How easy it is for the rights we enjoy to turn into duties. However, it is just as easy for the duties we have been given to turn into rights. If we were to win a large monetary award from some institution and were asked to travel somewhere to receive it, wouldn't we rush off happily to collect our prize, sacrificing our time and effort and making light of whatever difficulties we might encounter on the way? If so, then is not the prize of prayer worth the same effort, and even more? After all, how can the value of prayer even be compared to a reward that originates in this ephemeral earthly realm, however great it may happen to be?

God is the One who provides the birds with their nourishment. But they still have to spread their wings and fly to where it is. How would we ever know what a fruit tastes like if we never reach out to pick it off the tree? How can we enjoy restful sleep unless we make sure we have a suitable mattress and enough blankets, and that the atmosphere is calm and the room quiet and dimly lit?

4

The Satisfaction of Waking up early for Prayer

When I was a boy and I had to get up for the dawn prayer in the middle of the night - or so it seemed to me - I would wonder to myself why we had to get up at that particular time. First of all, I thought, if God wants us to offer Him five prayers a day, then why does He make one of them at such a difficult time and ask us to wake up just when we are enjoying such sweet slumber? What would be wrong with doing this prayer at seven or eight in the morning, or even at ten, for that matter? Isn't prayer still prayer no matter what time it takes place? Wouldn't the recitation we do during a prayer performed late be the same as the one we would have prayed at an earlier hour? And if the purpose of prayer is to preserve our communication with God and to drive Satan away, then what harm can Satan do us when we are sound asleep? Why should we be worried about losing our contact with God and being caught in Satan's snare at a time when we cannot think about any kind of contact or lack thereof, with God or anyone else, or plan out our actions, whether for good or for ill?

Questions like these might occur not only to children, but to adults as well. However, adults will realise in the end that Salah is not merely a matter of periodic communication with God Almighty, but a way of life. Whoever has experienced the sweetness of waking before dawn and going to the mosque, then leaving the mosque before sunrise to begin his daily work, of whatever sort it happens to be, will know the value of being an early bird, of breathing in the pristine breezes of daybreak, enjoying the tranquility of the early morning hours and the nearness one feels to God at that time.

Someone who does this witnesses the reawakening of life after its slumber as night gives way to day, the first threads of dawn steal forth, earth and sky emit a special glow, and the trees and flowers reveal themselves in the dawn's early light. A scene like this is a miniature reenactment of the first day of creation as signs of life make themselves visible all around. Those who have the privilege of experiencing this unique hour of the day will feel all their faculties opening up, blossoming, glowing with the desire to produce and give, and they will receive an inflow of strength, richness and creativity as though they had been given new life.

The dawn gives one a new eye through which to see the mysteries of the universe, and to discover the miraculousness of the creation in a way that would be closed to us at other times of the day. Whoever has tried waking up and working during the early hours of the day will find that two or three hours of work at this time are more productive than long hours of toil at all other hours of the day or night. And all that prevents us from benefitting from this special time is the devil of our own sloth. If we succeed in resisting and overcoming it for one day, followed by a second day, followed by a several-day period in the course of which we commit ourselves to this new pattern the way one commits oneself to fast during the first few difficult days of Ramadan, it will become an established habit in both body and mind, and such an enjoyable part of our daily programme that we will not want to do without it.

As we open our eyes whilst still in bed, Satan pulls our head toward the pillow saying, 'Close your eyes and go back to sleep. These early hours of the morning are the best time to relax and take it easy. So why be in a hurry to get up?' How can we resist Satan's repeated, insistent arguments, his alluring whispers? This is what the Messenger of God had to say:

> When one of you goes to sleep, Satan ties three knots around his neck. Then he tightens each of the knots, whispering, 'You've got a long night ahead of you, so rest!' If the person wakes up and remembers God, one of the knots will be untied. If he gets up and performs ablutions, another knot will be untied. And if he prays, all the knots will be untied, and he will begin his day energetic and in good spirits. Otherwise – that is, if he does not get up to pray – he will start his day sluggish and in a foul mood.[7]

Have you ever taken a close look at the faces of people who go to bed early and rise at dawn to pray? And have you compared them with the faces of people who stay up late, and then sleep through the dawn prayer? If you did, you would discover some of the secrets to this remarkable machine known as 'the human being', which has been programmed in such a way that the best time to restart it is before, not after, sunrise. This is how our Manufacturer designed us for some wise purpose – a purpose we may or may not be able to comprehend. However, who would know the secrets of this human machine better than the One who made it? 'How could it be that He who has created [all] should not know [all]? Yea, He alone is unfathomable [in His wisdom], aware!' (*al-Mulk* 67:14).

Nature springs out of bed at the first light of dawn, just as its Creator has programmed it to do, to illumine for us all the marvels of life around us. Hence, daybreak is not a time to sleep, but to rise, labor, produce and prosper the earth. Beware of underrating the value of this Divine gift, and of wasting the energy God has provided for us and other creatures around us to enable us to begin the new day. The flowers that close their eyelids at sundown open them again with the first dawn light, while the birds waken early, chirping and soaring through the sky in pursuit of their daily sustenance. Cows, sheep, goats, chickens, and all the living things God has placed on Earth meet the new day in the earliest hours to begin the cycle of life anew.

So, keep pace with life and reap its fruits before it is too late.

5

The Joy of Patient Perseverance

When we drive to our workplace or somewhere else, our concern is generally just to get to our destination, and at the fastest permissible speed (which we sometimes exceed!). Consequently, we arrive with minds exhausted, and nerves frayed.

But what if we treated our driving as though it were a right to be enjoyed? We would leave a little earlier than usual so as to have enough time to drive slowly and deliberately. As a result, we would have the chance to look at the scenery along the way, notice things we had not noticed on previous trips, and take pleasure in the act of driving and contemplating our surroundings rather than fretting about what time it is or what distance we still need to cover in order to get to where we are going.

When you go on a road trip, don't you set aside some extra time so that it will be more enjoyable for yourself and those with you? Don't you view the trip as a privilege to be indulged in rather than an onerous duty for you and your travel companions? This is the attitude we should adopt toward prayer as well.

The first thing to do is to conclude a brief truce agreement with Time. Within the framework of this agreement, you should be able to practice greater patience. In fact, you can make patience itself into a source of enjoyment. You may have experienced the enjoyment of exercising patience during the daytime hours of Ramadan, the satisfaction of learning to tolerate discomfort until it is relieved, patiently enduring illness until you recover, waiting good-naturedly in line for a ticket until you are allowed into a theatre or celebration hall, or disciplining yourself to study in order to succeed academically.

You may also have experienced the satisfaction of depriving yourself of something that you could have indulged in. For example, you may have refrained from buying a bar of chocolate, a new shirt, or a new car, in keeping with some principle, in faithfulness to a promise, out of modesty, or in a show of solidarity with others around you who could not afford to make such a purchase. This is what I mean by the enjoyment of patient endurance, which comes into play in the practice of prayer as well. As God commanded the Prophet, 'And bid your people to pray, and persevere therein' (*ṬaHa* 20:132).

Your patient perseverance in canonical prayer does not mean that prayer is a hardship, a test, or a punishment from God. Rather, it simply means that you exercise firm resolve and determination in order to obtain the sense of satisfaction you hope to achieve. The greater the potential pleasure or satisfaction, the greater the price, and the greater the patient endurance required. And could there be any greater pleasure than to confide our private thoughts and concerns to our

Creator and cast our worries and sorrows at His feet, and then emerge from this intimate encounter feeling purged of our sins and born anew?

Prayer is the School of Patience, and Patience is the School of Civilisation

I am baffled by the near-complete disappearance of talk on the virtue of patience from Western literature. One hardly finds any mention of it in Western discourse on the fundamental human virtues. This phenomenon has been confirmed by those who are more widely read than I am. There are discussions of courage, honesty, determination, industriousness, generosity, chivalry, cooperation, integrity, sincere dedication, love, justice, equality, freedom, democracy, humility, the willingness to help the unfortunate and needy, and many other praiseworthy traits. But, to my amazement, there seems to be little or no talk of the trait of patience even though it is foundational to all other moral virtues. When, on the other hand, I counted the number of times the Arabic word for patience, *Ṣabr*, and its derivatives occur in the Qur'an, I discovered they came to no fewer than one hundred and three, not to mention the hundreds of occurrences that one finds in the Prophetic Ḥadīth.

I say, 'to my amazement', because it is Western civilisation that has progressed tremendously in fields of scientific discoveries and inventions! We all know that patience is what enables the discoverer or inventor to work tirelessly day and night in a laboratory, engrossed in experiments of one sort or another and searching for new knowledge and applications. How could such individuals have achieved the progress they have without patience, persistence and determination? Given the outstanding scientific discoveries these people have made and their success in leading the world academically and in other areas, it may be that the virtues of patience, perseverance, and tenacity have taken such firm root in their character that they see no need to mention them in their writings.

If we look at the three principle forms of worship in Islam – Salah, fasting and the Hajj (pilgrimage) to Makkah – we find that each of them is a school specially designed to train us in patient endurance. You might say to yourself: It is clear how fasting and Hajj can teach us patient endurance. But what does patience have to do with Salah? If, as the Prophet taught us, Salah is only genuine prayer if it is performed with humble reverence and conscious presence, then clearly, patience is a vital element in its practice.

How easy, but how useless an undertaking it is, to rush absentmindedly through prayer to the extent that we do not even know what we are saying! Conversely, what a difficult, yet profitable enterprise it is, when we have countless engagements and tasks waiting at the door, to perform each recitation with deliberateness and presence. To utter an open-ended phrase such as 'God is greater' (*Allāhu Akbar*) and then, even with worldly business to attend to, pause to mentally fill in the hypothetical space that follows it (God is greater than who? Than what?) is a challenge that calls for a good deal of patience.

Similarly, to utter open-ended expressions of praise (such as *Subḥāna Rabbiyaa al-'Aẓīm*, I deem my Great Lord far above..., *Subḥāna Rabbiyaa al-A'llā*, I deem my Most Highly Exalted Lord far above...), and then, even with responsibilities weighing on us, to pause and mentally fill the hypothetical space that follows them (far above whom? or what?) calls for a good deal of patience.

Drawing out each word in the phrase *Bismillāh al-Raḥmān, al-Raḥīm* (in the name of God, the Most Gracious, Most Merciful, now and for all time) as the Prophet used to do so that we reflect on what it tells us about the Divine Character calls for a good deal of patience.

It takes a good deal of patience to pause after the phrases, 'greetings to God' (*al-taḥiyāt lillāh*), and 'goodly blessings' (*al-ṣalawāt al-ṭayyibāt*) in such a way that, despite all the commitments pending in our lives, we experience the joy of receiving God's response, to pause after greeting the Prophet in anticipation of his greeting in return, to greet 'God's righteous servants' (*'ibādillāh al-ṣāliḥīn*), and to give ourselves time to receive the reward for greeting all these individuals.

Lastly, and as we will be detailing below, it takes a good deal of patience to pause between each movement of prayer and the next, between each recitation and the next, between each verse of the Qur'an and the next, such that we give each of them the attention and respect it deserves in the midst of a busy schedule.

If you reflect on all your successes in life, all your accomplishments, and all your virtues, you are likely to find that what lies behind them is the practice of patience and determination. Conversely, if you think about your failures, your defeats, your sins and mistakes, you are most likely to find that what led to them was a lack of patience. What a remarkable school of success and salvation patience is, and what a remarkable school of patience prayer is!

Our gracious Prophet once said, 'The first thing that will be taken away from this community [the community of Islam] is humble reverence.' When humble reverence is absent from our prayers, so is patience, and when patience is absent, the Muslim civilisation declines. After all, God Almighty has affirmed the connection between our success and prosperity on Earth and our reverent communion with the realm of Heaven, saying, 'Truly, to a happy state shall attain the believers, those who humble themselves in their prayer' (*al-Mu'minūn* 23:1-2). So, after every one of the five daily prayers, ask yourself, 'How much "patience power" did I gain through the prayer I just prayed?'

6

Why do we Pray?

So why pray? Simply in order to learn patience? Why should we waste an hour or two out of every day performing strange movements and repeating phrases we have uttered hundreds of times before? Wouldn't it be better for us to spend this time helping others or doing some other kind of charitable or humanitarian work? What if Salah didn't exist?

Imagine what would happen if, all of a sudden, all wired and wireless communications were cut off, satellite stations ceased functioning, land lines and internet networks broke down, and all land, sea and air routes were closed off. Think of the anarchy, the frustration, and the economic, social, political and cultural collapse that would ensue.

A similar role is played in our lives by the communication between us and our Maker. So would we be able to do without it for even a single day? What would happen if the hotline between us and God were disconnected? If it were, we would have to invent for ourselves a way of staying in communication with Him. But would we be able to find anything better than the superbly formulated 'prescription' that we have in the Salah, with its carefully chosen words and its distinctive, expressive movements?

Prayer Reprograms Us

Just as the waves wear away at the boulders along the seashore with the passing of the days and the years, so also does life, by virtue of the

passage of time, familiarity, repetition and habit, wear away at the spiritual strength, equilibrium and inward purity we have achieved through prayer. Hour after hour, day after day, and year after year the earthly world works to program us in keeping with its fancies and whims. The process happens so gradually that we tend not to be aware that we have changed. In fact, however, we have drifted off the course set by our God-given inner compass, and we no longer conform to the original, 'virus-free' Divine program that had been installed in us. As the Messenger of God declared, 'The faith within you will grow old and tattered just as your clothes do. So ask God Almighty to renew the faith in your hearts.'[8]

By God's grace, and in distinction from the followers of other religions, we remain in possession of the original 'compact disc' that is, CD-ROM that contains the program for our faith. Consequently, we can refer back to it, adjust ourselves on the basis of it, and restore ourselves by removing whatever 'viruses' have crept in bringing distortion and maladies.

Word-for-word, authenticated narratives based on multiple sources and passed down by numerous narrators have given us the original template for the Salah as it was uttered and performed by the Prophet himself, who said simply, 'Pray as you have seen me pray.'[9] Now, if there were no Salah, would we have been able to 'invent' a prayer that would bring us into contact with the Majestic, Exalted Governor of the universe?

If we search the Hebrew Scriptures (the Old Testament) and the Gospel (the New Testament) in the existing form we have now, we find no details about the nature of the prayers that were prayed by either Moses or Jesus, upon them be peace, and that would serve as a model to be emulated by their followers. Hence, it is only natural that the followers of the Jewish and Christian religions would have invented certain prayers for themselves and passed them down from one generation to the next. However, those who perform such prayers lack the satisfaction experienced by Muslim worshippers based on the realisation that they are repeating a prayer that their Prophet once received directly from God Almighty.

As we have noted, neither the Old Testament nor the New Testament contains any detailed description of the prayers that were prayed by these two great prophets, and on which their followers can depend in their own prayers. In the New Testament, for example, we have a passage that describes how one of Christ's disciples said to him:

> 'Lord, teach us to pray as John taught his disciples.' And he said to them, 'When you pray, say,...' (Luke 11:2-4).

According to the account in the Gospel of Luke, the prayer Jesus gave his disciples consists of thirty-four words, while the Gospel of Matthew (Matthew 6:9-13) contains a version consisting of fifty-three words. A similar situation obtains in relation to fasting. Each denomination proposes its own conditions and rules for fasting, specifying which foods are allowed and which are disallowed, when and for how long one is to fast, etc. Moreover, such rules and provisions vary from one era to another, and from one country to another.

Muslims often get into heated arguments over small details relating to the Salah. Should we raise our hands, for example, every time we utter the words, *Allāhu Akbar* (God is greater)? Should we only raise them on some of these occasions? Or should we only raise them when we utter the opening Al*lāhu Akbar*? Where should we place our hands when we are in a standing position during prayer? Should we hold them over the navel? Above the navel? Slightly above that? The same types of arguments occur over other details of the Salah, which often leads to quarreling and alienation. When I observe such conflicts, I feel, believe it or not, a kind of gleeful satisfaction! After all, it is precisely because the form of prayer that has come down to us from our beloved Prophet via his Companions is so detailed and complete in its descriptions, based on numerous Hadith with exhaustive chains of narrators, that it is possible for such disagreements to arise. All the rulings we have in Islam descended from Heaven to Earth with the exception of those relating to prayer. In relation to this latter practice, the Lord of the Worlds chose to have his Messenger ascend to the heavenly realm to receive it directly from Him in its original, Divinely inspired form, and to return with it to Earth as a gift to the Muslim community.

What a faithful Prophet we have, one that brought us the gift of prayer just as he had received it from his Lord, and who took care to convey to us precise details on the easiest, most remarkable means of transportation in human history: one that transports us to the presence of God! Do we realise what a precious thing it is for us to have a complete, thorough picture of prayer exactly as it was received by our Prophet from his Lord during his miraculous night journey to Heaven, a picture whose broad outlines, and even some of whose minute details, are agreed on by all Muslim denominations?

Further, do we realise the importance of our having the Sunnah, which covers the details of everything in our lives through its description of virtually everything our Prophet said and did? No one will realise the importance of the Sunnah but those who comprehend what it means for other religions to be deprived of it. I marvel at, and pity, those who, unknowingly influenced by other religions, call upon the Muslim community to dispense with the Sunnah and to content themselves with nothing but the Qur'an!

What a treasure, what a distinction, what a source of protection and guidance it is that they want to strip away from Islam! God Almighty has made reference to the Sunnah in scores of verses in the Qur'an. He has called upon us to follow it, cling to it, and emulate the Messenger who brought it, saying, 'accept whatever the Messenger gives you, and refrain from anything that he withholds from you' (*al-Ḥashr* 59:7), and, 'pay heed unto God, and pay heed unto the Messenger' (*al-Mā'idah* 5:92). Indeed, obedience to the Messenger is, in essence, obedience to God: 'Whoever pays heed unto the Messenger pays heed unto God thereby' (*al-Nisā'* 4:80). Similarly, God affirms the relevance of the Sunnah to our lives and experience by speaking of it as 'a good example' (*al-Aḥzāb* 33:21).

Herein lies the importance of the Sunnah, which clarifies the critical nature of Salah and the necessity of performing it with all of its movements, recitations and other details. It is an original copy of a complete, intensive, Divinely inspired 'software' that acts to reprogram our souls five times a day. This number of repetitions is sufficient to eliminate any 'virus' that might infiltrate the 'computer' of our lives during the hours of the night or day. Prayer supplies us with a protective firewall against influences that threaten to distance us from our true selves and the path God intends for us. At the same time, it puts out the blazes of sins and grief that tend to break out in every corner of our earthly lives.

> You're on fire, you're on fire [from wrongdoing]! But if you pray the morning prayer, it puts out the flames. Afterwards you're set on fire again. But if you pray the noon prayer, the flames are quenched. Again you catch on fire, but if you pray the mid-afternoon prayer, the flames are put out once more. Still again you're set on fire, but when you pray the sundown prayer, the flames are extinguished. Still again you catch on fire, but if you pray the evening prayer, it douses the flames. Then you go to sleep, and nothing is recorded against you until you awaken.[10]

A young Japanese physician once asked me, 'Is it true that Muslims pray five times a day?' 'Yes,' I replied. In a tone of amazement bordering on indignation, she asked, 'How can you do that? Isn't that too often?' 'You're a doctor,' I told her, 'and in the course of your work, you meet with and treat large numbers of people every day. So, how many times a day do you disinfect your hands?' 'Somewhere between thirty and fifty', she replied. She looked at me, and from the look in her eyes I could see that she knew what I wanted to say before I had said it.

'Rise and pray, since in prayer there is healing.' [11] Life around us is filled with 'viruses' – temptations, deceptive allurements, human weakness, perversion and evil impulses. And the only thing that can cleanse us of such influences is not water, but prayer. Water cleanses the body of outward impurities, but prayer is the means by which you can purge yourself from within. If, after praying, you feel the same way you did before it, if you have no sense of something in you having changed, that you have rid yourself of some of the impurities and sins that had been clinging to you prior to praying, that you have been reborn somehow, then this means you did not make proper use of the prayer-based 'CD-ROM' for reprogramming, and that you will go back to thinking and behaving after your prayer in the same way you were doing before it.

If we compare the lives of those who pray regularly and from the heart with the lives of those who do not, we are bound to feel pity for the latter, since they lack a vital weapon for combating life's difficulties and enduring its many trials and tribulations. We will marvel at those who pray in the true sense of the word, as their faces remain full of light no matter how dark the road before them, while their eyes glisten with compassion, humility and meekness however harsh their trials. You can almost tell at a glance who prays truly and who does not. The Qur'an makes reference to this phenomenon when it speaks of those you see '...bowing down, prostrating themselves [in prayer], seeking favour with God and [His] goodly acceptance: their marks are on their faces, traced by prostration (*athar al-sujūd*)' (*al-Fath* 48:29).

The phrase *athar al-sujūd* has been rendered here as 'traced by prostration', thus implying that the phrase 'marks...on their faces' refers to the dark spot one sees on the foreheads of some people who spend a great deal of time in prostration. However, if this were what was meant by the aforementioned phrase, would not the verse rather read, 'marks...on their foreheads'? As I understand this phrase, it refers to the brightness one observes in such people's faces and the aura of kindness and magnanimity they exude. Such qualities, which are exhibited only by those who pray, will never be lost on a fellow believer.

In essence, all of the acts of worship required of a Muslim are simply means of reprogramming our souls, although they differ in their specific functions and temporal duration. The fast of Ramadan, for example, is a program that takes a long time to 'download' onto our souls; however, it also has long-lasting effects. Although the 'download' takes an entire month, its benefits extend over an entire year. By fasting, we 'reformat' earthly desires and cravings that had been intensified by 'viruses' over the course of the previous year. We reprogram our vision, which has inevitably been compromised over time by human weakness in the face of Satan's allures. Similarly, we reprogram our tongues which, as the months pass, have channeled a mixture of right and wrong, permissible and forbidden, good and bad, true and false. We reprogram our souls, which over the course of the year have been infiltrated by various pernicious maladies that have nearly killed the seeds of mercy, truth, justice, goodwill, contentment, humility, patience, righteousness, kindness, thanksgiving, faith and edifying discourse.

A similar function is performed by the Hajj, or pilgrimage to Makkah, albeit on a deeper, more enduring plane. The pilgrimage which is acceptable to God will be rewarded with Paradise, and those who perform it will, as the Messenger promised, be restored to the spirit of purity they enjoyed on the day they were born. Notice how the Salah grows gradually more frequent as the day progresses, and as life's pernicious assaults on us begin to escalate. After performing the dawn prayer (*Ṣalāt al-fajr*), we wait nearly half a day before performing the noon prayer (*Salat al-Duhr*). However, the time that passes between the noon prayer and the one following it is shorter, with the second half of the day being punctuated by the mid-afternoon prayer (*Ṣalāt al-Aṣr*), the sundown prayer (*Ṣalāt al-maghrib*) and, just over an hour later, the evening prayer (*Ṣalāt al-'Iishā'*).

Salah is designed to purge and reprogram the individual who prays. This, then, is one reason for its repeated performance throughout the day. And, I ask: Where, in any modern arms factory the world over, could you find a weapon this effective, this precise in its aim, this certain to hit its mark, and this certain to guarantee victory and achieve the desired outcomes?

7

The Rhythm of Prayer and the Rhythm of Life

In winter we seek out warmth; in summer, coolness. In sickness we search for a cure, in hunger for food, in thirst for water, in tumult for calm and tranquility, and in fear, for safety. When the wheels of life turn at an accelerated pace, which they most certainly do in this mechanistic, electronic age, and if our prayer is to be a refuge that prevents these wheels from crushing us between their sharp iron cogs, then it is only logical that the counterforce of prayer should offer the greatest possible degree of relaxation and serenity.

Have you ever imagined what would happen if Salah moved at the same harried pace that marks our daily activities? If this happened, prayer would turn into just another burden added to an already lengthy 'to do list', something that weighs us down, eats up our time, depletes our energy, and intensifies the pressure on our already pressured bodies and minds. And this is precisely what does happen in the experience of many. As a result, we try to be done with prayer as quickly as possible as we do with other laborious routines. In fact, given the discouraging outcomes we observe from the prayers we do pray, we might be tempted to dispense with this mechanical 'duty' altogether! And this is, in fact, what happens to many Muslims, who have no room in their lives for any more of this sort of frenzied activity.

I know full well that this change will be difficult for us at first. After all, how can we be expected to slow down in our prayers when a thousand and one tasks, responsibilities, appointments, programmes and meetings are clamoring for our attention? On the other hand, if this is how we are thinking as we prepare to take off into the lofty realms of prayer, our spaceship will never make it out of the earth's atmosphere and into outer space. Or, worse still, the spacecraft will go up in flames before it ever leaves the ground. We will be like the Muslim to whom the Prophet once said, 'Go back and pray again. You still have yet to pray.' [12] So, as we have suggested, prayer needs to serve as a counterweight to the hurried pace of our daily lives. Hence, it makes perfect sense for the prayers that involve silent recitation, such as the mid-afternoon prayer, for example, to be inversely related to the tone of life at that tumultuous time of day: a time of loud hustle and bustle when the sun is high in the sky and the temperatures are soaring, and amid the day's flurry of activity as people rush urgently about to accomplish their tasks and achieve material gain.

As for the sundown prayer, which is customarily accompanied by audible recitations, it bears a fitting inverse relation to the silence and stillness of the night as people retreat from striving to earn their daily keep and allow life's mill to turn at a gentler, quieter pace. Our audible recitation serves to fill some of the space left by life's unhurried tempo, and restores balance to our inner lives by reestablishing a harmony of sound, image and movement.

We conclude our day with the final evening prayer, which is marked by both length and variety. We perform four cycles of prayer (*raka'āt*), two of which are accompanied by audible recitations that counter the silence and stillness of the night, filling the space left to us by the retreat of the daylight hours by lifting our voices to God. The final evening prayer is followed by two Sunnah-based *raka'āt*, which are followed in turn by the Witr: one, three, five or some other odd number of *raka'āt*. This open-ended number, which is characteristic of many Islamic rituals of worship, provides us with a flexibility that allows us to extend prayer if we should feel especially weighed down by the burdens of the day, compromised by the day's events and thoughts, or in need of protection from spiritual assaults, temptations or struggles that we anticipate during the night hours.

Note that in general, the greater the number of obligatory prayer cycles at a given time of day, the greater the number of Sunnah-based cycles (that is, the prayer cycles that are not obligatory, but which are performed in emulation of the practice of the Prophet). This fact points to the need for the number of prayer cycles in each prayer to reflect the changes that take place in the conditions of our lives from one time of day or night to another.

8

Variety: The First Lesson in Civilisation

Have you ever wondered, as I have, why Islam's five daily prayers are of differing lengths, containing different numbers of cycles, movements, recitations and why they are required of us at different times? Why do they not all take the same form and last for the same amount of time as is true of the prayers performed in some other religions? Why this variety, these 'complications', these 'difficulties', these 'confusions'? Why do we perform different numbers of prayer cycles for the dawn prayer, the noon prayer, the mid-afternoon prayer, the sundown prayer, and the final evening prayer? Why are some prayers obligatory and others simply Sunnah (a voluntary emulation of the Prophet)? Why do some contain even numbers of prayer cycles, and others, odd numbers? Why do we have some Sunnah-based prayer cycles that come before the obligatory prayers, and others that come after them? Why are some Sunnah-based prayers referred to as 'highly stressed' (*mu'akkadah*), but not others? (Practices which are described as 'highly stressed' in Islam are those which the Prophet engaged in on a highly regular basis.) Why are some performed during the day, and others at night? Why are some recitations to be done silently, and others audibly? Why are some prayers performed individually, and others in community? The situation we have makes it look as though we are taking a difficult, high-level academic course that requires the worshipper to master a huge amount of material and complete the entire course before he or she knows how to pray. Doesn't this make things unduly difficult for children, minors and the uneducated? And does this make sense in view of the fact that Islam was revealed to a generally 'unlettered' nation of people who knew neither how to read nor to write?

Our limited human minds will never be able to fully fathom the Divine wisdom that underlies such matters; hence, we cannot arrive at answers to such questions on our own. However, as Muslims, we have been commended to think, to use our reason, and to explore God's wise purposes with respect to what He wills for us in the hope that, although we may not be able to grasp them in full, we might at least grasp them in part.

It has been a source of wonder to many, Muslims included, that at a speed even greater than that witnessed by the computer revolution in our time, Islam transformed the Arabs from a nation in which, if someone received a written message, he would have to travel elsewhere in order to find someone to read it to him, to a society that, in the space of fewer than two or three decades, established and developed the disciplines of linguistics with a focus on grammar and syntax, the writing of dictionaries, rhetoric, literary criticism, Qur'anic interpretation, variant readings of the Qur'an, the Hadith sciences, jurisprudence, biographies of the Prophet, criteria by which to assess the reliability of Hadith narrators as transmitters of the Islamic tradition and its narratives, geology, history, geography, philosophy, logic, medicine, astronomy, mathematics and numerous other academic fields.

The Islamic Salah played a role in the extraordinary rapidity with which Islamic civilisation came into being, a rapidity history had not witnessed prior to that time, and which it has not witnessed since. The challenging variety that characterises Salah in terms of its physical movements and recitations, the ways in which the recitations are to be uttered, the times at which prayers are to be performed, and the differing numbers of prayer cycles, or *raka'āt*, serves as the school in which the Muslim child's brain is first prepared to think, to memorise, to analyze, and to be inventive and creative. The activities involved in the Salah expand the power of children's brain cells, helping them to organise their thoughts, ramify questions and problems, categorise topics, and analyse data, thereby establishing the foundations of knowledge and preparing the way for the exploration of new cultural horizons. It was by means of this pedagogical mechanism that Islam was able to transform a race of unlettered people into what we would term, not an empire – since many are the empires that have known nothing but invasion, bloodletting and warfare, such as the Mongols and the Tatars – but, rather, into a fully rounded civilisation spanning the high levels of intellect, culture, the sciences and morals.

It is customary in the West for a child to begin school at the age of five. In most Arab and Islamic countries, children begin school at the age of six. However, Islamic schooling begins at the age of seven, since this is the age at which we have been commanded to teach our children how to perform the Salah. Given the rounded nature of Salah, every Muslim is expected to enter the school of knowledge, thought, culture and civilisation; thereby building at this young age-- with all that the term 'school' implies by way of responsibility, understanding, memorisation, preparation, and planning – the aptitude for success through excellence, inventiveness and creativity. Hence, there is to be no more illiteracy, no more ignorance, no more sloth, negligence, or capitulation to ignorance passed down from previous generations. You are Muslim, therefore, you are educated. You are Muslim, therefore, you are civilised.

The first subject one is expected to master and practice in the school of Islam is that of Salah. One memorises the number and names of the five daily prayers; their types (obligatory, Sunnah-based, etc.), their time periods, their recitations, their obligations, and the associated actions or movements that are permissible and impermissible. Then, in order to be a true Muslim, one must begin to put this knowledge into practice. It is not acceptable, once one has 'graduated' from the school of Islam, to forget what one has learned as so often happens in society when, after a student completes secondary school or university, almost nothing he or she studied and memorised is evident in his or her day-to-day life, since the degree he or she now holds is nothing but a way to get a job or make a living.

When Salah is joined with memorisation and recitation of the Qur'an, application of Qur'anic teachings to life situations, and memorisation of the things the Prophet did and said, young Muslims will tend naturally to study and absorb what they need of the other relevant Islamic sciences, which will enable them in turn to acquire a deepening understanding of other academic disciplines.

In the life of a Muslim, Salah embodies knowledge and culture; as such, it embodies civilisation. How else can one explain the fact that in many cases, students brought up to perform the Salah excel over those raised in households where the Salah is not performed?

However, in addition to planting the seeds of knowledge as well as culture in the worshipper, the variety inherent in Salah also performs another important function, and this is by inculcating an attitude of humble reverence.

THE IMPORTANCE OF VARIETY FOR HUMBLE REVERENCE

Anything repetitive, monotonous or mechanical will eventually cause us to lose our mental concentration, which will lead in turn to distraction, and possibly even put us to sleep. Have you ever noticed that when you drive down a long, straight stretch of the motorway, hardly ever varying your speed, tedium sets in and your mind is distracted? The number one enemy of humble reverence and the ability to immerse oneself in prayer and contemplate its meaning in such a way that one reaches God through it is capitulation to familiarity and habit. And this happens because we fail to make the best use of the variety permitted to us in Salah. We insist on taking the main motorway, as it were, rather than exploring the winding side roads with their constantly changing scenery.

The variety offered in Salah in the form of differing numbers of prayer cycles in each of the five prayers, the different times at which they are performed, the different forms of recitation involved, the varied bodily positions, the movement of the torso and limbs during prayer, and the way in which each type of recitation is associated with different positions and bodily movements, can help to reduce the possibility of our becoming distracted from what we are doing or saying when we pray, and spare us a sense of monotony and dullness. As a consequence, these features of prayer can make us more aware of ourselves, our actions and our words, more reverent, and more attuned to our connection with God as we perform this fundamental rite of daily worship. In addition, prayer is an excellent form of practical training for the brain which prepares it to absorb other lessons which have always been, and should remain, the foundation on which we build human civilisation.

The lessons to be gleaned from prayer are not easy ones. But when has it ever been an easy task to build human civilisations and establish states and polities? Such achievements can never be accomplished without a spirit of determination and commitment. Perhaps it is precisely because of the remarkable variety that marks the second pillar of Islam and the difficult lessons Muslim children are required to learn beginning at the age of seven that the Sustainer of the Universe chose to summon our great Prophet into His own presence at the lote tree in the Seventh Heaven in order to teach him this critical lesson rather than, as He did with other aspects of Islam, communicate it to him through the angel Gabriel.

Diversity is a means of teaching flexibility and acceptance of others. The Prophet has taught us invaluable, unforgettable lessons in flexibility and variety, whether through the Salah or through other means, and particularly through the voluntary, or Sunnah-based prayers. This flexibility epitomises the spirit of tolerant, moderate Islam, which adapts itself readily to different eras and environments, and to varied communal and individual circumstances.

WHY SO MANY DIFFERENT POSITIONS AND MOVEMENTS?

As we are beginning to see, the varied bodily positions entailed by the Salah are not arbitrary. Otherwise, we could simply recite everything in our prayer while seated, standing, reclining or lying on our backs or fronts, as in the prayer performed by someone who is weak or infirm, for example, rather than being obliged to engage in physical movement.

Apart from the role played by prayer's physical movements in helping us to avoid the dangers of repetition, monotony and distraction, we might well ask: Why are the various recitations in prayer accompanied by changing bodily positions? Why is the phrase *subḥāna rabbiya al-'ẓīm* (I deem my Great Lord far above...) uttered during the bow, for example, rather than during the prostration, during which we utter the words, *subḥāna rabbiyaa al-a'lā* (I deem my Lord the Most Exalted far above)? Why is it only during a standing position in Salah that we utter Qur'anic verses, whereas it is only while seated that we utter phrases passed down based on the non-Qur'anic text? And the 'why's' go on.

The changing positions we adopt during Salah can, as we have seen, help us to remain wakeful and vigilant, lending full attention to the One to whom we are addressing ourselves. As our varying bodily postures are linked with our recitations, we are trained through prayer in how to internalise the content of what we are reciting, while our bodily movements are an affirmation of the words that come out of our mouths. As such, they uphold the intimate link between our speech and our actions, and our complete confidence and faith in what we are saying or reciting. Regardless of how we interpret the prayer's bodily positions, they nevertheless harmonise with the words we speak, and this harmony reflects our desire to draw near to the One we are addressing.

Also, worthy of note in Salah is the worshippers' commitment to facing the qiblah and keeping their eyes on the spot where their foreheads touch the floor during prostration, their strict insistence on looking neither to the right nor to the left while refraining from responding to, or even looking at, anyone who speaks to them during prayer for any reason whatsoever, and treating the region between them and the qiblah as 'sacred space' through which no one is allowed to pass. All these practices put others on notice that when in prayer, the Muslim enters into a special state of 'set-apartness' in which no worldly concerns should be allowed to interfere.

9

The Call to Prayer and its Ten Wonders

Allāhu Akbar, Allāhu Akbar, Allāhu Akbar, Allāhu Akbar!
Ash-hadu an lā ilāha illā Allāh! Ash-hadu an lā ilāha illā Allāh!
Ash-hadu anna Muḥammadan rasūl Allāh, ash-hadu anna Muḥummadan rasūl Allāh.
Ḥayya 'alā al-zakāh, ḥayya 'alā al-zakāh!...

God is greater! God is greater, God is greater, God is greater!
I bear witness that there is no god but God. I bear witness that there is no god but God!
I bear witness that Muḥammad is the Messenger of God, I bear witness that Muḥammad is the Messenger of God.
Come to zakāh, come to zakāh!

Have you ever heard a call to worship like this one? Neither have I! It is one I made up in an attempt to jolt myself, and you, out of the daze of familiarity that deprives us of the ability to hear or recite the text of the *adhān*, or call to prayer, in the way it was heard and recited by Bilāl Ibn Rabāḥ, Islam's first muezzin, the very first time he sounded the call to prayer so long ago.

Both the *adhān* and the *iqāmah*, or the announcement that communal prayer in the mosque is commencing, have suffered the effects of over-familiarity and habit and their tendency to rob us of the value of the spiritual treasures at our disposal. However, the content and wording of these two recitations, as well as the unique role played by each, conceal marvellous wonders. In what follows I will attempt to identify ten of these wonders, there no doubt being numerous others that I, with my limited human capacities, have yet to discover.

First: Has any of you ever stopped to wonder why it is that of the five pillars of Islam, only Salah is preceded by a special 'announcement'? The *adhān* is a public invitation to engage in this vital pillar of our religion. So why do we not issue a similar public call to commence the fast of Ramadan? And why do we announce in the *iqāmah* that we are about to commence communal prayer, whereas we issue no such announcement before commencing the month-long fast of Ramadan, or our distribution of zakāh, as the imaginary *adhān* cited above?

We lack the ability, through human insight alone, to grasp the Divine wisdom that has singled out Salah for these two 'introductions,' the *adhān* and the *iqāmah*. We can, however, discern the semantic importance of the *adhān*, which reminds Muslims – and how easy it is to forget – that the obligation to perform the Salah is not a private, individual matter, something that we perform alone and independently of others. Rather, it is, first and foremost, a communal, shared act. The *adhān* is an affirmation of the communal nature of Salah, and an invitation to the members of the community to gather and perform it together, at the same time, in the same place, and behind a single prayer leader. It serves to emphasise that the role of Salah is not limited to the relationship between the individual and his or her Lord, but includes the act of meeting with others, drawing close to others, cooperating with them, standing (literally) shoulder to shoulder, and fostering mutual understanding and affection between the individual servant of God and other members of the Prophet Muhammad's faith community. This is why the Sunnah-based, voluntary prayers, which are generally performed individually, need not be preceded by either the *adhān* or the *iqāmah*.

This, then, is one of numerous culturally-related aspects of the Salah about which we will speak in greater detail below in the section entitled, 'Communal Prayer: The Secret to Civilisation'.

Second: The story of how the *adhān* and the *iqāmah* came into being has a miraculous aspect to it that might be said to elevate them nearly to the status of Divine revelation itself. Their verbal content was communicated through dreams, not to the Prophet himself, but to two of his Companions. Both men had the same dream, on the same night, including exactly the same words and details. Yet more important and exciting still is the fact that one of the two Companions involved was 'Umar ibn al-Khaṭṭāb, the second of the four rightly-guided caliphs.

The distinctive manner in which the *adhān* was 'born' is matched only by the manner in which Salah itself came into being, the latter of which brings into even greater relief the uniqueness of the *adhān* and the way it came to us. With the exception of the Salah, the content of the entire Qur'an was communicated via Divine inspiration. In the case of prayer, the Messenger of God received a supernatural invitation to the heavenly realm to receive this rite in all its details from the Lord of the Worlds, who, as we have noted, delivered the *adhān* to His Prophet through the dream that was given simultaneously to two of his faithful Companions.

Third: In structure and meaning, the *adhān* is essentially a brief introductory prayer that prepares the believer for the lengthier prayer to follow. We know from the example set by the Prophet that one is to recite the *adhān* into a newborn's ear as if to prepare him or her for a lifetime of prayer. It is as though the *adhān* were saying to the child, 'Now that you have entered this world, prepare yourself to begin a lifetime of prayer, worship, and nurture of a spiritual communion with God that will continue beyond your existence in this world. In fact, when you die, you will set out on another, never-ending journey with God that differs from your short sojourn on Earth.'

The Qur'an tells us that the details of our earthly lives are actually nothing but an act of worship that takes a variety of forms. God Almighty declares, 'And [tell them that] I have not created the invisible beings (jinn) and human beings to any end other than that they may [know and] worship Me' (*al-Dhāriyāt* 51:56). When you study and learn, you are at prayer. When you work to support yourself and your family, you are at prayer. When you serve society and other individuals, you are at prayer. When you eat to live and maintain your strength, you are at prayer. When you take care of your health, you are at prayer. Our whole lives from A to Z are, in essence, a means of worshipping and praying.

Take a close look at the words of the *adhān*, and you will find that it is simply an abridged prayer that prepares the way for a longer, more detailed act of worship.

Fourth: Suppose now that you had never heard of the *adhān* or the words that make it up. Imagine you were hearing the phrase Allāhu Akbar (God is greater) for the very first time even though in reality, it is older than the *adhān* itself (the expression had been familiar to the Muslims since their receipt of Salah from the Prophet after *laylat al-mi'rāj*, or his night journey to the heavenly realm). Reflect on its meaning and its singular linguistic form. Grammatically, it is an incomplete statement that, depending on your imagination and/or circumstances, could be finished in numerous possible ways: God is greater...than the earthly realm that distracts me from Him. God is greater...than my material possessions. God is greater...than the worries that disturb my peace of mind. God is greater...than the enemy I am facing. God is greater... than the bullies and tyrants who persecute me.

The phrase *Allāhu Akbar* (God is greater) sums up the entire call to prayer. It is the focal point of this extraordinary call that marks Islam uniquely among the religions of the world. In fact, it encapsulates Islam itself. We are 'Muslims' because we have declared our surrender (*istislām*) to a Being greater than we are, the Being that is greater than all else. We have surrendered, turned ourselves over, to this Being. Hence, the phrase *Allāhu Akbar* might rightly be referred to as the watchword that sums up all that Islam is.

Fifth: The Islamic call to prayer, brief though it is, embodies a unique linguistic style that was new both to the Arabs of the Prophet's time and to other communities and nations. Its style was centuries ahead of its time. Note, for example, that it consists of a series of brief, staccato statements that are not held together by any of the connecting particles that are generally used between one phrase and another, such as 'and,' 'so', and the like. It is reminiscent of the style we tend to use in the text messages we exchange nowadays on our mobile phones. With its succinct, direct phrases, the *adhān* summed up for the Muslims of the Prophet's day the spirit of the new message for whose sake they had abandoned their idols, previously held doctrines and their ignorant ways.

Sixth: More remarkable still is the fact that with its rapid-fire linguistic style, this concise prayer corresponds to the language of the most important part of the Salah, that is, the *Fātiḥah*, or opening *sūrah* of the Qur'an. Like the *adhān*, the *Fātiḥah* is devoid of the various linguistic connectors that Arabs, like others, are accustomed to seeing and using. If the *Fātiḥah* had been written in a style more similar to everyday human speech, I suspect it would read something like this (with my additions in square brackets):

> [We lift up] praise to God, [who is] the Sustainer of the worlds [and who is also], the Most Gracious, the Dispenser of Grace, Lord of the Day of Judgment. [Hence, O Lord, we have come to affirm that] You alone do we worship; and unto You alone do we turn for aid [in all the affairs of our lives. Hence, we address ourselves to You, asking and beseeching You to] Guide us (to) the straight way....

Seventh: Given the position the *adhān* occupies in Muslim worship, certain protocols and rules of etiquette are associated with it. In keeping with the example set by the Prophet, we are to reply to the words of the *adhān* with specific phrases. Have you ever heard of interactive computer systems and the various other remarkable devices and systems based on the same concept? Our relationship with the Islamic call to prayer, as demonstrated by our gracious Prophet fourteen centuries ago, is an interactive relationship between the muezzin and his hearers. For every phrase uttered by the muezzin there is a corresponding phrase that his listeners are to 'echo' with certain words of response.

Eighth: One element of the striking linguistic correspondence between Salah and the *adhān* is a dualistic structure whereby each of its component phrases is repeated twice. This duality affirms the *adhān's* autonomous linguistic character while, at the same time, affirming its harmony with the overall structure of Salah.

The number two is not a widely occurring number in Islamic rites of worship, recitations and litanies. More commonly appearing numbers are three, seven, ten, twenty-seven, thirty-three, ninety-nine and a hundred. Nevertheless, the phrases of which the *adhān* is composed are repeated twice, a phenomenon that corresponds to the dual structure of Salah, as when we raise both hands when uttering the opening *Allāhu Akbar* (known as *takbīrat al-iḥrām*), adopt a sitting position after each two prayer cycles, or *raka'āt*, perform two prostrations as part of each prayer cycle, and conclude the prayer with two greetings of peace, one to the angels on our right, and the other to the angels on our left. These features of the Salah further confirm the sense that, as we repeat the *adhān*, we are actually reciting a brief Salah.

Ninth: You may have noticed that the words of the *adhān* are neutral in terms of person, number and gender in that they involve no use of the first person (I/we), second person (you), or third person (he/she/they) pronouns. The only exceptions to this pattern are the two 'testimonies', which stress personal responsibility and the importance of affirming this responsibility by the speaker in the words, 'I bear witness that there is no god but God. I bear witness that Muhammad is the Messenger of God.' Even the command translated as 'Come...' (*ḥayya*) in the phrases, 'Come to prayer, come to prayer! Come to salvation, come to salvation!' contains nothing to mark it as singular or plural, masculine or feminine and, hence, is devoid of the limitations that tend to be embedded in everything we say and write. This particular linguistic style occurs only rarely, being associated primarily with praise (*tasbīḥ*), litanies of Divine remembrance (*adhkār*), and canonical prayers (*Ṣalawāt*). However, the entire first half of the *Fātiḥah*, the backbone of Salah, is marked by this same infrequently used, neutral style.

Tenth: There may be some who view the sounding of the call to prayer as a marginal practice that does not merit the attention generally given to Salah. Such individuals are likely to think of the *adhān* as unimportant, and consequently, neglect to utter it before performing the Salah. However, the Messenger of God, who was a faithful bearer of the message he had received from on high and who, in the words of his Lord, was 'full of compassion and mercy towards the believers' (*al-Tawbah* 9:128), said otherwise. He declared, 'Should any group of three worshippers fail to sound the *adhān* or the *iqāmah* amongst themselves, Satan will get the better of them.'[13] Similarly, ʻAbd Allāh ibn ʻAbd al-Raḥmān ibn Abī Ṣaʻṣʻah related on the authority of his father that Abū Saʻīd al-Khudrī had once said to him, 'I see that you love your sheep and goats, and that you love being out in the desert. When you are tending your sheep and goats, you are at prayer. So, raise your voice in issuing the call [to prayer]. For whatever jinn, human being, or any other creature hears the voice of the muezzin making the call to prayer will testify in his [the muezzin's] favour on the Day of Resurrection' (narrated by al-Bukhārī).

So, one might ask: If the *adhān* were nothing but a means of drawing other peoples' attention, what need would there be for sheep, goats, the desert and inanimate objects to hear it? And how does Satan get the better of people among whom the *adhān* is not sounded? Although we may not know exactly how this takes place, such declarations by our gracious Prophet shed light for the early Muslims on the value of both the *adhān* and the *iqāmah* and the role they play in nurturing a worshipful spirit in our lives. So, do your best not to allow these expressions of worship to escape from your grasp.

If I were asked today, 'How many kinds of Salah are there?' I would reply, 'Silent, spoken and public (by the latter I refer to the *adhān*)'. Each of these three types of prayer has a different role to play, and each of these roles is equally important, complementing the others in helping us to manage our lives and correct ourselves when we err.

The *adhān* might be described as an abridged, preliminary investment project that prepares us for the greater, final investment project: that of Salah.

10

The Two Ritual Ablutions

> But for the fact that I loathe to impose a burden on my people, I would instruct them to perform a *wuḍū'* (ritual ablution) before every prayer, and with every *wuḍū'* to clean and polish their teeth with a small stick.[14]

I used to pause at this saying of the Prophet and wonder: Why 'before every prayer'? As long as I maintain ritual purity, which is at the heart of the Prophet's example, why would he want me to perform my ablution all over again? Supposing I did perform it again even though I was already ritually pure, wouldn't this be a waste of precious water? And it seems especially strange for such an exhortation to have come out of the heart of the desert rather than i.e. out of the land of the great lakes and falls!

I have read both the Jewish scriptures, and the Christian scriptures, as well as the Muslim Scripture, and as many of the Hadith collections as I can. Through this reading I have seen that neither Judaism nor Christianity links its doctrines, rites of worship and overall culture with ritual purity, washing, and ablutions as much as Islam does. Nor have I ever read of a prophet who instructed his community to maintain hygiene and cultivate a pleasant appearance as much as the Prophet Muhammad did. However, the Muslim community's practices are a far cry from what their Prophet exhorted them to follow.

Islam's emphasis on the repetition of ritual ablutions is due not only to the fact that cleanliness is a sign of health and advanced civilisation, and is thus a clear aim of Islamic law. It is due also to the fact that, exemplified here in the ritual ablution, good hygiene is associated with inner purity. The purity of one's body and clothing are a natural outgrowth of one's inward purity, which will reflect itself automatically in one's outward demeanour. Hence, some Islamic juristic schools include backbiting, for example, among the actions that invalidate one's ritual ablution.

By this logic, it might be said that there exist two kinds of ritual ablution, inward and outward, with the inward being more important than the outward. In fact, outward ablutions will be of no use to someone who lacks inward purity. After all, what good would it do someone sinking into a pit of excrement to perform a ritual ablution? While you wash your outer limbs, you should make certain that you have done whatever it takes to cleanse your inner being. Such inward cleansing is not accomplished with water, sand or any other material substance. Rather, it takes place as we rid ourselves of the 'grime' within, be it hatred, envy, rage, slander, selfishness and egotism, trickery, impiety, ingratitude, ill-will, sharpness of the tongue, meanness, disobedience, mistrust or duplicity.

Make it your intention to be cleansed of all such impurities, if even only gradually. In this way you should become able to surrender your heart, your mind, your spirit, and your words, to God Almighty. Moreover, when you stand in God's presence on the Day of Judgement (and it won't be long in coming), your words will find acceptance with Him, He will listen to your quiet supplications, and your sins will be forgiven.

> A man once came to the Prophet (pbuh) and said, 'So-and-so prays at night, and the next morning he goes out to steal.' To this the Prophet replied, 'What you are saying [that is, the fact that he has prayed] will prevent him from stealing.'[15]

> Once the Prophet asked his listeners, 'Do you know who the bankrupt person is?' To this they replied, 'The bankrupt person is someone who has no money or possessions.' And he told them, 'Rather, the bankrupt person within my community is one who, on the Day of Resurrection, presents God with the prayers he performed, the fasts he kept, and the charity he distributed, but who also is found to have cursed, insulted and physically abused others, stolen their wealth, and shed blood without good cause. As a result, his good deeds will be distributed among the people to whom he did harm in this earthly life. Then, if his good deeds run out before his bad deeds have been compensated for, these other people's sins will be taken and cast upon him, and he will be cast into the fire.'[16]

How many Muslims are 'bankrupt' in the sense of which the Prophet spoke? How many of us have allowed worship to become disconnected from our daily practice? We may see someone bowing and prostrating, his forehead bearing a dark spot indicating the frequency with which he holds it to the floor, only to find that in our dealings with him there isn't a trace of mercy, consideration or kindness. The Qur'an tells us that 'prayer restrains [man] from loathsome deeds and from all that runs counter to reason' (*al-'Ankabūt* 29:45). The phenomenon of disconnecting worship from daily practice poses a serious danger to the image Muslims project to the world of their Islamic faith. No such separation was allowed by the Prophet himself, who taught the Qur'an's contents and their application side by side.

> Ubayy 'Abd al-Raḥmān al-Sulamī narrated on the authority of 'Uthmān, Ibn Mas'ūd and Ubayy Ibn Ka'b that the Messenger of God (pbuh) would recite ten verses of the Qur'an to them, and that before they went on to the following ten verses, he would have them learn how to apply the ten they had just learned. Hence, they would learn the teachings of the Qur'an and how to apply them at the same time.[17]

We need to rediscover our rites of worship. We need to rediscover Salah. And whenever we find deadly familiarity dulling our senses to the greatness of this uniquely Islamic expression of reverence, we need to rediscover ritual ablution. Try performing the ritual ablution as though you had just learned of it, and as though you were performing it for the very first time. Then ask yourself: What did I discover through this experiment? If you examine yourself carefully, you will find that like Salah, ritual ablution embodies an entire way of life.

Firstly, it signals an emphasis on cleanliness and orderliness, which are marks of culture, education and civilisation. Secondly, it reflects care, deliberation and perseverance, qualities that set the successful apart from the unsuccessful. Thirdly, fourthly, fifthly, and ...tenthly, cleanliness points to a steadfast, insistent process of self-examination and the desire to be rid of whatever impurities you may have acquired since your last ritual. It also sets the believer apart from the unbeliever, the God-fearing from the godless, the repentant from those who are still wandering about lost. You may even be able to distinguish those who have performed the ritual ablution from those who have not by looking into their faces.

The rite of tayammum, or sand ablutions, might be likened to a 'wireless' (read: waterless) communication to the heart that says, 'Prepare to meet God, and rid yourself of everything that might spoil your imminent encounter with Him.' After all, as the Omniscient Sovereign, God is apprised of all your secrets, equally cognizant of what you conceal and what you reveal. As for the usual ritual ablution, it is an 'aqueous' message that communicates the same messages to the heart, only in a different way.

The Arabic word *wuḍū*", translated as 'ritual ablution', is derived from the same root as the word for 'light' (*ḍiyā'*) since it illuminates both the face and the heart. After all, the light radiated by the face is simply a reflection of the light that comes from the heart and the soul.

Try always to be in a state of ritual purity. If you do, you will feel as you walk to your workplace as though you are floating on air. When you greet others, you will feel as though you are shaking hands with the angels. As you go about your daily tasks, you will feel confident of success. And as you lay your head on your pillow, you will be blessed with a sense of having fulfilled your responsibilities for the day to the best of your ability, and that at long last you have placed yourself in the hands of the most Trustworthy, the most Generous, the most Forgiving, the most Merciful.

11

Communal Prayer: The Key to Advancement and Civilisation

Have you ever tried to define the term 'civilisation'? Does it refer to factories, computers, missiles, marine and air fleets, spaceships and atom bombs? All of these things are among the fruits of civilisation. But as for civilisation itself, the source of these fruits, it might be said to grow from the following ten 'seeds': (1) cleanliness, (2) precision and mastery, (3) punctuality, (4) organisation and self-discipline, (5) honesty and integrity, (6) teamwork, (7) tolerance, humility, and acceptance of others, (8) specialisation and individual responsibility, (9) patience, ambition and determination, and (10) justice and equality.

Have you ever asked yourself, as I have, why communal prayer is necessary? Why are we required to leave our homes, offices, businesses or factories five times a day at a very specific hour, so specific, in fact, that if we are just five minutes late, we will have missed the worship? Have you ever asked yourself, as I have mine, why we are expected to look our best when we go to the mosque? Why we have to purify ourselves ritually beforehand? And why the ritual ablution? Does it have to do simply with respect for the house of God, or with the cleanliness without which we won't be duly prepared to stand in God's presence? Or, alternatively, does it have to do with the cultural functions performed by purity, good hygiene, personal adornment and orderliness as expressions of respect and propriety, functions which have their counterpart in the religious or spiritual domain?

With regard to punctuality, we find that communal prayer serves as the best school a Muslim could possibly graduate from as a fully qualified torch-bearer of civilisation. As I have noted, being as little as five minutes late for the communal prayer means that you miss it, and lose your claim to the reward you would have received for attending on time. This situation, which repeats itself five times a day in a Muslim's life, is bound to teach him the value of time, and the importance of being punctual in his engagements with others.

Once, when I was a young man, I engaged in a lively discussion with Shaykh al-Albani in which I defended the idea of permitting more than one session in a single mosque for a single communal prayer. Why, I asked, is it not permissible for worshippers who were late to the first session of a group prayer to choose a prayer leader from among themselves and perform it together in a second session? And why not, after this, allow a third or fourth group to do the same?

Shaykh al-Albani was adamant in his rejection of my proposal. Unfortunately, it was not until much later that I understood the wisdom in his position. Allowing multiple different groups to hold separate sessions for a single communal prayer in the same mosque simply gives free rein to divisions within the congregation; a multiplicity of directions, a multiplicity of factions, and disunity, alienation and fractiousness outside the mosque. Conversely, commitment to praying with a single group or congregation provides daily, ongoing training in punctuality, adherence to a set meeting time, unity, solidarity and group cohesion.

As for ritual purity, proper hygiene and maintaining one's appearance, all of which prepare us to enter the mosque and to stand in God's presence, they are the same things that prepare us for the transition from the darkness of ignorance i.e. 'uncleanness'-- meaninglessness, backwardness, apathy and neglect -- to membership in the 'club' of civilisation, which closes its doors to those who fail to meet its basic conditions in terms of cleanliness, neatness, and attractive, appropriate appearance not only on the level of personal hygiene and apparel, but in their mosques, homes, offices, schools and hospitals.

It was Islam that first introduced the Arabic word for mosque, masjid, which means 'a place of prostration'. Appropriately, the term masjid is reminiscent of the position in which we are closest to our Lord, that is, an attitude of prostration in which the head, the forehead and the nose are touching the floor or the ground. Such a posture expresses the profoundest degree of humility and brokenness. Hence, the more you abase yourself before God with your physical being, the nearer you draw to Him, and the higher your station in His presence in the life to come.

When believers come reverently into their Maker's presence every few hours of the day and night and engage in such training in humility, never being 'too proud to worship Him' (*al-A'rāf* 7:206) as God Almighty says of them and His angels, humility becomes such an established part of their nature that there ceases to be any place in their lives for arrogance or petty disagreements. Rather, they come to be 'humble towards the believers' (*al-Mā'idah* 5:54) in keeping with God's command to His faithful Messenger to 'spread the wings of your tenderness over the believers' (*al-Ḥijr* 15:88). When we conduct ourselves in this way, we have taken our first step toward entering the realm known as 'civilisation'.

When we enter the mosque, we remember that we are entering the school of prostration, the school of humility, meekness, brokenness, and tenderness toward fellow believers. Another, equally common, Arabic name for mosque is *jāmi'*, or the 'place that gathers'. We remember as we enter it that this is the place that brings us together, makes us equals, unites us, and eliminates hatred and bitterness from our hearts and minds. As a consequence, there are no more quarrels and resentments, and no more distinction between young and old, lowly and great, indigent and wealthy, commoner and royalty, oppressed and oppressor.

> Keep your rows straight, for you are lining up as with the angels. Stand shoulder to shoulder and fill in the gaps [in your rows]. Deal gently with your brethren to ensure that you leave no breach through which Satan might steal. When you draw close to each other in your rows, God will draw close to you, but if you draw away from one another, God will draw away from you. [Narrated on the authority of 'Abd Allāh Ibn 'Amr, and declared authentic by al-Albānī in Ṣaḥīḥ al-Jāmi'.

How many times have we read this exhortation from the gracious Prophet, or heard it quoted in conversations or Friday sermons? How many times has it been repeated to us by an imam as prayer is about to commence in the mosque?

Yet how many of us have stopped to ponder its every phrase, to read between its words and lines? If we did, we would realise that this injunction is more than simply a rule concerning standing in straight rows. It is a recipe for reforming souls, and for creating a civilised society whose members are all equal and in which no one lords it over anyone else.

When we stop to reflect on this saying of the Prophet, the first question that comes to mind has to do with why so much importance is placed on making the rows of worshippers straight, and on having them stand shoulder to shoulder. What is so important about worshippers standing in straight lines and keeping their shoulders and feet neatly aligned? And the answer, quite simply, is: because this is where civilisation begins. This is another one of the 'seeds' of a civilised society.

We are invited to attend this gathering for prayer, since civilisation is not an individual undertaking, but a communal one. It is based on teamwork and the relinquishment of egotism and selfishness. A civilisation is, first and foremost, a community.

Secondly, we are invited to keep this precise, specific appointment not just once, but five times a day with our brothers or sisters. In this way the spirit of commitment and punctuality will begin to flow through our veins. Culture, after all, is founded on rigor, commitment, and respect for both our own time and that of others.

Thirdly, we are urged to form rows with the other members of the community, since our orderliness in this context will translate into greater orderliness in our inner lives, mastery in our work, and unity in our hearts, all of which will help give rise to a thriving, cooperative, civilised society. Civilisation arises out of collective effort, integration, order, mastery, patience, humility, tolerance, acceptance of the other and solidarity on the levels of means and ends alike.

Not content to allow this instruction to be sabotaged by our human frailties, the Prophet linked it directly to the heavenly realm. It is as if he were saying: 'Remember, all of you who stand in God's presence, that these rows of yours as you pray on Earth are modelled on the rows of angels in Heaven.' When he told his listeners, 'you are lining up as with the angels', the Prophet was drawing a link between the building blocks of civilisation on Earth and what takes place in Heaven. In brief, what this Hadith tells us is that sound worship equals sound civilisation, and that as worship is in Heaven, so also should it be on Earth.

Additionally, we are called upon to adhere to another condition, that is, to 'fill in the gaps...leaving no breach through which Satan might steal.' In so saying, the Prophet was drawing attention to the role of credibility and personal responsibility in the creation of a civilisation. With whatever special capacities we possess, each of us stands at a certain frontier of our community. Each of us has his or her own individual role to carry out, his or her own individual action to perform, and his or her own unique skills to employ toward shaping civilisation. If we abandon our responsibility to 'fill in the gaps', whichever gaps they happen to be, it will leave a 'breach' in our protective wall. Consequently, such an abandonment constitutes an act of treason that leaves the community vulnerable. In sum, civilisation is founded on specialisation, individual responsibility, and cooperative, constructive effort.

Once again, the Prophet links this earthly instruction to Heaven, as if to say: 'O servants of God: If you join ranks in prayer in this world, God will embrace you in the next, but if you break ranks here, God will leave you in the lurch there.' ('When you draw close to each other in your rows, God will draw close to you, but if you draw away from one another, God will draw away from you.') What clearer connection could there be between the conditions of human civilisation here on Earth, and what takes place in the realm of Heaven? In short, the conditions for sound worship are themselves the conditions for a sound, healthy society.

And above all we are called upon to eschew all harshness and cruelty and to treat our brothers and sisters with gentleness in prayer, in society, and in life as a whole. As the Prophet said, 'Deal gently with your brethren.' In other words, when others attempt to close the gaps in a row of worshippers, we should facilitate the process by making room for whoever needs to shift this way or that, close a gap between two rows, etc. Doing so on a regular basis will shape our characters in such a way that we no longer tend towards harshness or rudeness, militancy, extremism or violence in our thinking, in the disposal of our affairs, or in the way we respond to those who hold opposing points of view or doctrines. This is the example that was set for us by the Messenger of God in all aspects of his life. As Ā'ishah, Mother of the Faithful, once related:

> ...He [the Messenger of God] never struck either a servant or a woman. In fact, he never once struck anything with his hand unless he was engaged in combat in the way of God. Whenever he was given a choice between two different courses of action, he preferred the one that entailed the least hardship – provided, of course, that this action involved no sin. If it was sinful, he would shun it entirely. Nor did he ever

> avenge himself on anyone for any reason whatsoever unless one of God's sacred commands had been violated, in which case he was avenging not himself, but God.[18]

Alas, the Messenger of God urged us to be humble, but we have been arrogant. He taught us to be gentle, but we have been cruel. He demonstrated moderation and tolerance, but we have exhibited harshness and extremism. He exhorted us to live with mutual understanding and to draw near to each other, but instead we have quarrelled and drawn away from one another. He taught us to come together and unite in strength, but we have been divided and weakened.

Sunni and Shīʿah Muslims have differed over numerous details of faith and practice. However, never once over the centuries have they disagreed over the essentials of Salah, the number of prayers per day, the movements they involve, or the times when they are to be performed. And the reason for this lies in the communal nature of offering prayer.

The communal structure of most of Islam's rites of worship has protected them from distortion. Muslims have never differed over the text of the Qur'an because Islam requires them to recite it communally and to verify its correctness during each of the three daily prayers whose recitations are performed aloud (the dawn prayer, the sundown prayer and the final evening prayer). This process takes place in every mosque, in every country of the world, in every village, in every home: the prayer leader recites, while those worshipping behind him check and, if necessary, correct, his recitation. However, Muslims have disagreed over the Qur'an's interpretation, since exegesis is not a communal practice. They have not differed over the form of Salah because it is a public rite which is confirmed in the mosque by the congregation as a whole, five times a day; however, they have differed over the One to Whom hearts are first directed in the prayers, since God alone can observe what is in our hearts. Similarly, there has been no disagreement over the form or foundations of the Hajj, or major pilgrimage, since, like Salah, the pilgrimage is a public rite that is performed under the watchful eye of the entire Muslim community. However, there have been differing emphases among Muslims on certain aspects of the Hajj as opposed to others.

If we attempted to identify the qualities that characterise societies that have become more civilised versus those that have remained backward, we would find that those who have become more civilised are those that have demonstrated humility and tolerance, unity and cohesion, those who have developed areas of specialised knowledge and expertise and worked to build up their homeland as a single team, with one heart and spirit, with determination and enthusiasm, while those that have remained backward have exhibited arrogance, pride, harshness and rigidity, and been neglectful of their duties towards each other, each of them going his own way such that if two factions come together, they only come together to quarrel or fight. Does not this latter description, alas, fit most Muslim societies in the world today?

The Messenger of God said, 'If there are three people in a given village or rural area who fail to perform the Salah together, Satan is bound to get the better of them. You must take pains to perform communal prayer, because the wolf will devour the sheep that becomes separated from the flock' (narrated by Abū Dāwūd on the authority of Abū al-Dardā'). If we gave careful thought to this saying of the Prophet and applied it to ourselves, our families, and others around us, the reason for the Messenger of God's emphasis on communal prayer would be clear: It is through communal prayer that we acquire and maintain strength and cohesion. Otherwise, like sheep that have strayed from the flock, we will be easy prey for the wolves of which there are so many in this world.

When our hearts, and not just our bodies, come together in the communal prayer, this unity is bound to be reflected in our daily lives and our way of thinking. We will begin to act not just as individuals, but as a group. Our preferences will be guided not by our individual propensities, but by the interests of the group. What we accept or reject will be determined not by individual tastes and desires, but by those of the group. We will think together, work together, build together, rejoice together, grieve together. Only in this way were Muslims able to go from the ignorance, backwardness and decadence of the pre-Islamic era to the moral and intellectual refinement of the Islamic era that followed, including the territorial expansion and unity that were achieved under the early caliphs. Indeed, Heaven and Earth were united for them when they united in prayer in the hope of Paradise. As the Messenger of God declared, 'Be steadfast in communal prayer, and beware of allowing yourselves to be divided. Satan draws up behind the individual alone, but steers clear of two who are together. Whoever wishes to have a spacious, comfortable abode in Paradise should pray in community.'[19]

Civilisation is founded upon the practice of regular assembly, of integration, unity, mastery and precision, modesty, compassion, tolerance, acceptance of the other, rapprochement, enthusiasm, dedication, determination and patience.

12

The Friday *Khutbah* (sermon): A Course in Development

The congregation in a certain mosque in Oxford were in an uproar after their imam gave his sermon entirely in English. 'The sermon isn't valid, since it wasn't in Arabic!' they objected. 'The whole *Jumu'ah* prayer will be unacceptable if the sermon wasn't delivered in Arabic!'

Here in Britain, we may find ourselves baffled and amazed at such an incident. At the same time, we can not help but feel admiration and appreciation for these brothers of ours who, though they do not speak Arabic, exhibit a reverence, love and respect for the language that we, its native speakers, have lost. The sentiment on their part is so intense and heartfelt that it puts us to shame. It serves as a wake-up call by stripping us bare of the negative, deadening effect of over-familiarity on our respect and love for our mother tongue, and helps us to reconnect with such emotions and rediscover the sacredness of our language and the special place it merits in our lives.

This is the bright side of the aforementioned reaction on the part of our non-Arab brothers. There is, however, another, dimmer side to their response. These brothers' insistence that the Friday sermon be delivered in Arabic and in no other language, even if they don't understand a word of what the imam says, points to a distorted, inadequate understanding of the role the Friday sermon is intended to play in Muslims' lives. It also highlights the dangerous split that exists for some Muslims between their religion and their day-to-day reality. Such individuals' attitude seems to be: As long as you deliver your sermon in the language of the Qur'an and the Prophet, it doesn't matter what you say or don't say. And as long as you perform the five daily prayers required of you, it's fine for you to steal, cheat, lie or commit sexual immorality. Be sure not to eat pork or any other meat that is not permitted under Islamic law; then sin however you like!

The image non-Muslims have formed of Islam, particularly in the West, reflects the warped thinking and practice of Muslims themselves, who so often focus on matters of marginal importance while losing sight of their religion's essentials. Just think of the injustice Muslims do to Islam through their lack of understanding!

These brothers of ours stipulate that their imam's Friday sermon be in Arabic rather than, for example, their local language, or some other language they understand. The sermon might consist of no more than a few verses from the Qur'an, a smattering of Hadiths, and some pithy sayings that the imam is accustomed to repeating in every sermon he preaches. Then the worshippers leave the mosque virtually in the same condition in which they arrived, with nothing learned, no new understanding acquired, no wisdom gleaned, no benefit gained, no remembrance of God rekindled, no clarification of legal rulings based on the Scripture and no treatment of pressing modern-day issues. In this way we Muslims kill the spirit of the Friday sermon, leaving nothing but its linguistic shell.

We rob this important weekly didactic opportunity of its meaning, turning it into nothing more than a mindless verbal ritual. Similarly, many Muslims rob their rites of worship of their practical significance by divorcing them from their day-to-day lives. They pray and steal; they fast and lie; they perform the pilgrimage to Makkah and then proceed to cheat, commit injustices, backbite, trample on others' rights, and transgress God's law to their heart's content. In this way they perpetuate a bizarre sort of disconnect between their spiritual and practical existences.

This being the case, you might find someone lecturing you on the need to observe certain rules pertaining to halal meat, even if you happen to have your own, more correct approach to the question of which meat is halal and which is not. Moreover, this very individual may be someone who, whether secretly or openly, lives the life of a conniving imposter, a cheater and a liar, a thief, a rancorous man who willingly bears false witness against his neighbour, and who skirts the law every chance he gets. He might even be a drug user. Yet in spite of it all he thinks of himself as a model Muslim. This is the best-case scenario. In the worst-case scenario, he is liable to declare you an apostate unless you abide, rightly or wrongly, by his definition of halal meat.

The aforementioned description applies to an unfortunately broad sector of today's Muslims. Their unspoken motto is: Pray, then do as you please. Say whatever you want in your Friday sermon, since all that matters is that it be in Arabic. Do whatever you like and treat others however you wish to, since all that really matters is for you not to eat anything but halal meat in keeping with our provincial, inadequate notion of 'halal'.

Many Muslims are unaware of the fundamental role played by the Friday sermon in the growth and development of an Islamic society. Consequently, they treat the Friday prayer and sermon as though they were simply ritual duties that have to be performed. So, when they attend the prayer, they feel satisfied with the fact of having relieved themselves of an unfulfilled duty. They show up on time, listen to the imam, line up behind him in straight rows and perform their prayer, and that's that!

It behoves us to ask, then: Have we been exhorted to listen to the imam who gives the Friday sermon and to remain quiet and still while he speaks simply out of politeness and respect for the speaker? If so, doesn't this mean that the Friday prayer is little more than a religious ceremony involving certain bodily movements and exercises whose content is of no importance, and whose content has no meaning? The Salah is an expression of worship, and the Friday sermon is a plan of action. The sermon is an organic, inseparable part of the Friday *Jumu'ah* prayer. Hence, some Hadiths treat someone who misses the sermon as though he had missed the prayer:

> On Fridays the angels are stationed at the mosque door, recording and classifying people according to their various stations. 'So-and-so came at such-and-such a time. So-and-so came at such-and-such a time. So-and-so arrived after the imam had started to preach. So-and-so came in time for the prayer, but missed the sermon; hence, he missed the Friday prayer.' [20]

An imam who wants his listeners to come away from the Friday sermon with something meaningful should tailor his words to the needs, interests, circumstances and educational level of those in his congregation. Hence, a sermon preached to a congregation of labourers will have to be different from one addressed to a congregation of intellectuals, to a congregation of school students, to university students and professors, to new converts and so on.

When preaching, the Prophet never repeated Qur'anic verses in a haphazard, disjointed fashion after the manner of many modern-day imams, whose sermons amount to little more than a few verses or Hadiths that they parrot repeatedly to their congregations without any attempt to connect them to contemporary reality. We do an injustice to the verses themselves when we repeat them mindlessly to people without any meaningful context. Such a practice can have a negative impact on worshippers' morale and attitudes, turning their love for these Hadiths and Qur'anic passages, and possibly others as well, to dislike and alienation.

When will a sermon's rhetorical style become less important than its content? When will the matter of eating halal meat be treated as a secondary issue in comparison to the fundamental moral teachings of Islam? When will our lives become an embodiment, an application, and a confirmation of our acts of worship? If as we have been informed by our gracious Prophet, God sends someone to revive the Muslims' religion for them once every hundred years, then the role of the imam in his Friday sermons is to breathe new life into the rulings of our religion on the specific situations and problems we face from one week to the next so that we can keep pace with life's ongoing movement and contribute to its evolution and development.

Just as every educational institution has a mandatory training and development programme for its workers and staff, the Friday sermon is the training, development and guidance programme required in the life of a Muslim, the official weekly link on the levels of knowledge and practice between the institution of Islam and the institution of life.

This is where we begin

I once went to check on a brother who had stopped praying at our mosque. I had been told that he had started attending another mosque because he was at odds with a particular member of our mosque. Then I met up with another brother who had not come to the mosque for quite a while. 'So,' I asked him, 'why don't we see you at the mosque any more?' He replied, 'I don't want to pray in a mosque whose imam teaches that human beings were created from a "despicable" drop of sperm. How dare he refer to the drop of sperm we came from as "despicable"?!' Some time later as I was on my way to the mosque, I ran into a Muslim friend of mine and we got into a conversation. When we reached the mosque, he bade me farewell, clearly not intending to come in. Surprised, I asked him, 'So aren't you going to pray with us?' Shaking his head, he replied, 'I don't worship in mosques where Salafis pray.'

And I thought to myself: What will become of us if everyone in the Muslim community belongs to one of these three groups: those who refuse to pray in the same mosque as someone they have had a disagreement with, those who refuse to forgive a preacher or imam for a human error - assuming that the case in point was, in fact, an error; and those who are not willing to worship with anyone who disagrees with their religious opinion or interpretation? Do you think a community like this will be qualified to govern itself some day, still less the whole world?!

What has become of mosque protocol? What has become of the rules of etiquette that once governed communal prayers? What has become of the historical role once played by mosques, which served as springboards for people who brought Islam to the world with unparalleled speed, forging a golden age of learning and Islamic civilisation, and spreading morals throughout the world?

In April, 2012 I was invited to participate in a course which was being organised by an institution in Egypt known as the Academy of Contemporary [Muslim] Preachers. The course was to be held in Cairo for the stated purpose of 'highlighting examples of outstanding Azhar graduates, both academically and behaviourally, to communicate the message of moderate Islam to today's youth.'

Based on my experience of nearly two decades as an inspector for the British Accreditation Council, whose work was expanded recently to include universities and institutes outside the United Kingdom, I have proposed the establishment of what I term the 'International Islamic Accreditation Council'. The purpose of this council would be to create cultural centres which are subject to the conditions of this new council in various Arab and Islamic countries. The first of these centres would be established in Egypt; however, they would not be restricted to universities and other educational institutions, but would include all state institutions, both large and small, including firms and governmental bodies, government bureaus, streets, small neighbourhoods, residential buildings, hospitals, clinics, schools, institutes, clubs, department stores, mosques, churches, public parks, children's parks, public bathrooms, workshops and so on.

The fifty students who had participated in the course organised by the Academy of Contemporary Muslim Preachers, who came from a variety of Egyptian provinces, would form the nucleus for this idea through small local organisations linked centrally to the aforementioned accreditation council. Institutions in the region would then be encouraged to compete for the council's recognition in the areas of religion and culture, and institutions that had not applied for such recognition or accreditation would find themselves isolated from their surroundings.

It was hoped that the aforementioned centres and sites would spread over the months and years, and that they would exert a growing impact on various aspects of life in Egypt with the result that within one or two decades, Egypt would find itself on a par with European nations in terms of skill, order, discipline, cleanliness, appearance, productivity, workplace safety, educational levels and interpersonal relations. All of this, of course, would help to restore the country to the religious values it had lost sight of.

When the idea failed to get off the ground due to the unfortunate events that followed the revolution of 25 January 2011, we began thinking of an alternative direction, namely, of beginning from the smallest cultural unit in the Islamic state: the mosque community, of which at least one will be found on every street, in every neighbourhood and in every village. Each mosque, headed by its imam and a group of its regular attendees, can be transformed into a kind of local accreditation council for the institutions within its immediate geographical area. Its evaluations of such institutions would be based on the ten basic cultural conditions which we proposed above in our discussion of communal prayer.

The criteria for recognition by the British Accreditation Council – beyond those which apply specifically to universities – are applicable to any group operating within the state, and may be summed up as follows:

1) The building's external and internal appearance.
2) Health, safety and cleanliness conditions for its workers and those who benefit from its services.
3) The appropriateness and readiness of the physical structure, including its offices and other rooms, for provision of the kinds of services which the institution offers.
4) Availability of the insurance needed for all workers and beneficiaries.
5) The administration's success in running the institution and achieving its aims.
6) Properly documented staff qualifications, including the level and quality of the degrees they hold, and the appropriateness of the experience they bring to their work.
7) Ongoing staff training courses.
8) Regular contracts for all the institution's employees, and a just, equal pay scale.
9) An incentives system that encourages individual initiative on the part of workers and develops their talents and gifts.
10) An efficient, modern system for organising records and files for staff and beneficiaries.
11) Clearly stated and well-preserved bylaws, regulations, policies, plans and job descriptions for all employees.

12) Credible advertisements, announcements and publications.
13) Provision of credible and reliable services, experience, expertise and degrees.
14) The use of civil, appropriate language, written or spoken, in addressing others.
15) The administration's communication with employees and beneficiaries and its responsiveness to their opinions and demands.
16) Facilities provided by the institution to its staff and beneficiaries, particularly those with special needs.
17) The degree of equality accorded to staff and beneficiaries and the absence of racial, tribal, partisan, or doctrinal discrimination among them.
18) Participation by external referees in an annual assessment of the institution's activities and services.
19) Assessment of the outcomes achieved at the end of each semester/ year/phase, etc.

This, then, is the list of categories and criteria to which an inspector must give attention when visiting an institution seeking recognition by the British Accreditation Council. They are all basically consistent with the ten 'seeds' of civilisation identified in an earlier discussion, seeds that are planted and nourished by communal prayer.

A movement growing out of communal prayer might begin in scattered mosques. Then, based on the ten categories mentioned earlier each mosque would set criteria that must be met by any institution or organisation that seeks to be accredited. At a later stage, bodies representing the participating mosques could meet to form a unified council and to agree on a set of standardised criteria.

These standardised criteria could then be developed and expanded into a constitution or set of bylaws for a National Accreditation Council that operates on the level of the state.

Initiation of such a movement would have to be preceded by a well-designed plan on the part of one or more imams, who would work to form a community of worshippers united by an awareness of the true function of communal prayer and its role in daily life and societal reform. This initial, founding community might form the nucleus of a larger community comprised of the congregations of all the mosques in a given region. This larger, more inclusive community would then constitute the Higher Accreditation Council.

Whether in Egypt or some other Muslim country, such a movement would then be set to spread all over the Muslim world. Given the proper planning and execution, such a movement could, within a matter of a few decades, restore the Muslim community to the place it once occupied among the civilisations of the world by reviving the spirit of sound religious reflection and by linking Islamic rites of worship to both private and public life on the practical level. In this way, Islam could reveal its true cultural face to the rest of the world.

It promises to be a big task. However, the longest of journeys begins with a single step, and if we approach it with the needed seriousness and resolve, we can hope, by means of such a council, to achieve what generations of governments and thinkers have failed to accomplish.

13

The Five Lines of Prayer

> O you who have attained to faith! Do not attempt to pray while you are in a state of drunkenness; in order to know what you are saying. (*al-Nisā'* 4:43)

How many times have we recited this verse of the Qur'an, yet without discerning the lessons it holds for us? If you happened to see a man walking down the street talking, gesturing with his hands and nodding or shaking his head, yet without seeing anybody beside him, the first thought that would occur to you would be that he must be talking to someone on a mobile phone in loudspeaker mode, or with headphones in his ears. If, on closer inspection, you discovered that he had nothing in his ears, no microphone near his mouth, and no mobile phone in his hand or his pocket, you would have to conclude that he was crazy, senile, or drunk. Or am I exaggerating?

The analogy applies to how we perform the Salah. When you look at someone praying and you see no one beside them, no mobile phone in sight, addressing apparently thin air with no one in front of them at all, this can be a powerful image if done right. In Salah we can either be connected inwardly with God or, if oblivious of Him, act little differently to those speaking out loud without a microphone or mobile phone, who appear drunk, unaware of what they are saying.

There is a significant difference between speaking in such a way that it is apparent from our posture and the expression on our face that we mean what we say and that we are engaged in a conversation, and simply moving lips and tongue giving the appearance that we are talking to someone or that we mean something by what we say. The latter situation involves a hurried recitation of words that originally had meaning, but which, given the speaker's expressionless demeanour, dull facial features, and the monotone in which the words roll off his or her tongue, no longer communicate anything of significance.

Right now, try taking your phone and calling up a friend. Ask your spouse or some other family member to record every time there is a change in your facial expression, your tone of voice, or your manner of speaking during the ensuing conversation. Our features, the rate at which we speak, our tone of voice, our hand gestures, and our bodily positions change over and over again in the course of a normal conversation as we give and take; we request, insist and demand; we accept and reject; we plead and we praise; we object and protest; we reproach and caution; we register surprise and disappointment, dismay and relief; we question and answer. We express amazement and hesitation, dread and anticipation. We make judgements, we offer affirmations and denials. There are pauses and resumptions, corrections, hesitations and so on and so forth. If none of the above takes place as we speak, it means we are nothing but robots.

When you perform the Salah, have you ever tried to make certain that you do not seem like a robot, a drunkard or a lunatic? Have you worked consciously to ensure that 'somebody' is actually contacting 'somebody' the way one of us would contact a friend, a professor or a superior at work? Have you ever stopped to think about how you can tell that there is a real live person on the other end of the line? If you are confident that God really is 'at the other end of the line', that you are addressing Him and that He is listening, that He is remembering you as you remember Him, and that He responds to your supplications, then what evidence of this could be observed by someone who happened to be watching you or listening to you as you pray? In fact, how can you prove to God Himself, Who hears your every tone of voice, counts your every heartbeat, and knows your every thought, that you are actually speaking not to 'nobody', but to Him?

> Truly, to a happy state shall attain the believers: those who humble themselves in their prayer. *(al-Mu'minūn* 23:1-2)

> Woe, then, unto those praying ones whose hearts from their prayer are remote. (*al-Mā'ūn* 107:4-5)

Any moment of contact with God, even if it is devoid of speech, is better than reams of text that we recite without any communication taking place. God Almighty looks at our inward beings. So, to address God wordlessly for a single moment from the heart is better by far than to address

Him endlessly with words, but without the heart's echo – assuming, that is, that we really do want to reach God and, through our communication with Him, to reprogram our souls, find the way to happiness, and wipe away the sins that have stained our spirits.

> And be constant in praying at the beginning and the end of the day, as well as during the early watches of the night: for, verily, good deeds drive away evil deeds. (*Hūd* 11:114)

Prayer is not a kind of physical exercise, although it does involve physical activity. It is not simply the time we set aside for its performance, even though its performance does take time. It is not merely words we form with our lips and tongues, although they are a part of it. Rather, Salah consists of five simultaneous, interconnected, integrated lines, and if we want our prayer to involve true communication with God Almighty, none of these lines should be viewed as self-contained, independent of the others. They are not mentioned in the sacred texts among the pillars of prayer. Nevertheless, they constitute the most essential elements of all since prayer would not be prayer without them.

The 'lines' of which I am speaking are: (1) time, (2) the tongue, (3) the body, (4) the heart, and (5) action.

Time: Do not try to convince me or yourself that within the space of five or six minutes you can finish the noon Salah, the mid-afternoon Salah, or any of the other required Salah prayers of the day. The amount of time you devote to worship is a matter of fundamental importance in determining whether prayer, or communication with God through prayer, has actually occurred. Perhaps the most important part of the time factor in prayer are the moments of silence that intervene between one verse and another, and possibly even between one word and another. Avoid letting the words crowd onto your tongue, with each of them in a rush to get ahead of the next. Savour them, rolling them around on your tongue like honey. To every sentence, every phrase, even every word of your prayer, devote a few moments of silence during which you can turn it over in your mind and reflect on its meaning. Relish its beauty. Make certain that your mind has not wandered, and that you are taking in its meaning as you utter it. Let half your prayer be taken up by silence, and half of it by quiet conversation directed to God alone.

The tongue: With the tongue we recite the words modelled for us by the Messenger of God, seeking to do justice to each word and each meaning with the appropriate intonation, melody and volume. It is only by virtue of the needed harmony among all these elements that the worshipper will experience full presence and true humble reverence.

The body: Our entire demeanour, from our gestures to our facial expressions, has a role in expressing the meanings of the words we are reciting. The face, the eyes and the whole body convey the meanings of the words even if our tongue and lips make no movement. Have you ever observed the prayers of someone who lacks the ability to speak? He pours all his powers of expression into his eyes, his face and his body in order to compensate for his inability to express himself verbally. Learn to pray with your body as if you were mute. Then reinforce your bodily expressions with your words.

The heart: The heart should beat to the movement of the tongue such that each of them confirms the truthfulness of the other. One's thoughts and preoccupations should not be in one place while one's lips and tongue are in another.

Ideally, the words we utter with our lips should find some kind of physical expression. If only the interaction between the heart and the body were such that at the sound of words that moved us inwardly, tremors went through us, our faces went pale, our voices quivered, or tears welled up in our eyes!

Action: We should form a conscious intention to let our daily lives be a practical application of the words we utter and the emotions we experience during prayer. Our lives should be the physical embodiment of the words we utter in worship. The Salah should not be a mere formal ritual that bears no connection to our daily practices and our relationships with God and others. Just as ritual ablution has both an outward aspect and an inward one, so also does prayer. In both the Qur'an and the Hadith literature prayer is linked to action, application, commanding what is good and forbidding what is evil.

> 'O my dear son! Be constant in prayer, and enjoin the doing of what is right and forbid the doing of what is wrong....' (*Luqmān* 31:17)

> Yet they were succeeded by generations [of people] who lost all [thought of] prayer and followed [but] their own lusts; and these will, in time, meet with utter disillusion. (*Maryam* 19:59)

> If your prayer does nothing to deter you from the commission of actions that are harmful and contrary to reason, then it does nothing but take you farther from God.[21]

Hence:

- Pray with your limbs as though you had no face.
- Pray with your facial expressions as though you had no tongue.
- Pray with your tone of voice as though you had no body.
- Pray with your heartbeats as though they were your last beats.
- Prolong your prayer as though you were praying for the last time.

A certain man was invited to attend a large celebration in a far-away land. So, he put on his best clothes and undertook the long, arduous, costly journey to the place where the celebration was to be held, passing up opportunities for worldly gain in the process. When at last he reached his destination, he produced the invitation he had received and was allowed entrance into the festivities. Once in the great hall, he sat down among the other guests and waited for the events to begin. But within minutes, even before the curtain was raised, the man had dozed off in his seat! Some time later, the man awoke suddenly to the sound of servants asking him to leave so that they could clean the celebration hall. The party was over, and the guests had dispersed and gone home!

This man is like those of us who, in response to a Divine invitation, prepare for prayer by performing the ritual ablution, then spend whatever time and money we need in order to get to the mosque. Then spend some time at the mosque in worship. After all this, however, we leave without having experienced any of its spiritual blessings, without feeling any connection with our Maker or receiving the reward we had hoped to.

The Messenger of God once helped two Muslim men befriend each other. Then one of the two men was killed, and the other was killed a week later. After the second man's death, some in the Muslim community said, 'O Lord, forgive him his sins and cause him to join his friend [in Paradise]!' To this the Messenger of God responded, saying, 'How could this man's prayers be compared to his friend's? How could his good works be compared to his friend's? They were as far removed from one another as Earth is from Heaven!'[22]

Just think: If one week's worth of Salah can earn you such an immense Divine reward, then imagine the reward you can obtain by a single prayer! Take another look at this incident and what the Prophet said in response to it. He was not content simply to ask, 'How could [the number of] this man's prayers be compared to his friend's?' Rather, he followed it with a question that is inseparable from the first, saying: 'How could [the number of] his good works be compared to his friend's?' Hence, this Hadith is a reminder to us that prayer and action are an organic unit, and that neither should be divorced from the other.

Every time you finish praying, ask yourself: How far did the prayer I just performed lift me? Did it lift me above the heavens? Beyond the moon? Past the clouds? Over the roof of my house? A few hand spans above my head? A couple of inches? One inch? None at all?

Never leave the mosque after prayer without making sure that you are a different person than the one who came in a few minutes earlier.

14

Red Key No. 1: 'God is Greater'

Allāhu Akbar

As we saw before, the phrase, *Allāhu Akbar*, 'God is greater,' conveys a unique energy that empowers us to distance ourselves from the earthly realm. However, the instance of this phrase that we utter at the beginning of the Salah, known as takbī*rat al-iḥrām*, or 'Divine praise of consecration', has an even more special quality about it, as it ushers us into a sacred realm comparable to the state of consecration into which the pilgrim to Makkah enters before undertaking the Hajj.

If someone said to you, 'The enemy is weaker,' then fell silent, what would you think? You might say to yourself: What comes next? Why didn't he finish his sentence? Or: Maybe he suddenly felt unwell, or something prevented him from finishing the phrase. Since you would have expected the person's statement to take a more complete form, all these explanations might suggest themselves to you. You might have expected the person to say, for example, 'The enemy is weaker than we had supposed'. In other words, one would expect the word 'weaker', as the comparative form of the adjective, to be followed by 'than...'. Instead it has been left open to many possibilities, rich possibilities that allow the listener or speaker to finish it in the privacy of his own mind with scores, or even hundreds or thousands of alternative endings: God is greater...than you, Satan! God is greater... than you, O tyrant! God is greater...than you, O worries of mine! God is greater...than you, O pleasures and delights of the world! God is greater...than anything that might distract me from talking or thinking about the One who is the Author of all.

The Arabic adjective used in this phrase (*akbar*) means neither 'great' nor 'the greatest' but, rather, 'greater'. However, given that even we Arabs have failed to understand it rightly, blinded as we are to the stultifying effect of familiarity and repetition, it should come as no surprise that those rendering it into other languages have often made the mistake of translating it as 'God is great,' or 'God is the greatest' rather than maintaining the distinctive ambiguity and open-endedness of 'God is greater'.

If you listen carefully to muezzins and to those who issue the announcement that communal prayer has begun (the *iqāmah*), you will find that most of them elide the two repetitions of *Allāhu akbar* such that they actually say, *Allāhu akbarullāhu akbar...* as though it were a single phrase. In so doing, they rob the first *Allāhu akbar* of its distinct character, and we fail to hear it for what it really is – an open, incomplete phrase followed by ellipses (Allāhu Akbar...) that we are invited to complete with our own imaginations.

This merger of the two separate instances of *Allāhu akbar* is one of numerous practical outcomes of the fact that, by virtue of excess familiarity, we have lost touch with the distinctive linguistic nature of this phrase. We have turned it into an ordinary sentence devoid of any open-ended elements. So, who can blame translators who mistakenly render *Allāhu akbar* as 'God is great' (*Allāhu kabīr*) or 'God is the greatest' (*Allāhu huwa al-akbar*)?

Try to imagine yourself among the residents of the city of Madinah when they heard the very first *adhān*, or call to prayer. How would they have felt as they encountered this new, unfinished linguistic structure? *Allāhu akbar... Allāhu akbar... Allāhu akbar....* Time and time again they heard the word akbar, 'greater,' yet without hearing the grammatical complement they would naturally have anticipated.

Allāhu akbar – the phrase with which we begin every Salah – might thus be likened to the first in a series of 'red buttons' which you press as you board prayer's cosmic 'spaceship' before it soars with you into the furthest reaches of the celestial spheres.

15

Reading, Reciting and Chanting

A Muslim brother once asked me, 'Why don't we plan out what we're going to recite during the Salah? How is a passage that reads, for example, 'And the divorced women shall undergo, without remarrying, a waiting-period of three monthly courses' (*al-Baqarah* 2:228) going to help us come closer to God or be more humble or reverent in His presence?'

In fact, when reciting from the Qur'an, we have to bear in mind that we are not reciting human speech, but a Divine revelation. We are not reciting in the ordinary sense of the word – that is, in the sense of simply uttering a text aloud. Rather, we are emulating, or following, the recitation done before us by the Messenger of God, who in turn followed the recitation done before him by the Angel Gabriel, who in turn had followed God Almighty.

The Arabic word rendered 'emulating' or 'following' here, *tilāwah* (derived from the verb *talayatu*), is a word used specifically and solely in reference to the recitation of the Qur'an. Prior to the Qur'an's appearance, the desert Arabs had not been familiar with the use of the verb *talā* in such a linguistic context. To them the word simply meant 'to follow' or 'come after.' They might say, for example, 'A man came in to where we were seated and was followed (*tal'hu*) by another.' In the Qur'an, by contrast, this verb was used in the sense of emulating or following someone else in the act of recitation. When, in our day, we recite the Qur'an ourselves, we 'follow' (*natlū*) the Messenger of God, who 'followed' the Angel Gabriel, who in turn had 'followed' his Divine Sustainer, Exalted be He, in reciting the words of the revelation.

Can you see the importance of this point? We are engaged in an ongoing process of 'following' God Almighty Himself. As we recite verses from the Qur'an, we experience a sense of direct, warm, intimate connection between ourselves and God Almighty via this sacred chain of which we are now one link. So, as you recite passages from the Qur'an, be aware of the place you now occupy in this noble chain.

The rules of formal, melodic Qur'anic recitation, or *tajwīd*, have played a significant role in ensuring the Qur'ān's faithful, accurate transmission down the ages. As such, with its processes of assimilation (*idghām*), prolongation (*madd*) and abridgement (*qaṣr*), separation (*faṣl*), connection (*waṣl*) and pauses (*waqf*), we have been trained in perfect precision and absolute fidelity in our circulation of the text. As a result, our present-day recitation is an exact replica of the original recitation or reading which Gabriel received from his Lord and conveyed to the Messenger of God, and which the Messenger of God in turn conveyed to us.

The rules of *tajwīd* teach us to give our recitation more time than we would to an ordinary reading of the text aloud. This additional time helps us to digest the meanings of the Qur'anic verses and the individual words that make them up, since we are not allowed to pass over them in haste without connecting the movement of tongue and lips on one hand, and the movement of our thoughts and imaginations on the other. Try reciting the last *sūrah* of the Qur'an, entitled *Sūrat al-Nās*, without adhering to the rules of *tajwīd*. Then go back and recite it while applying these rules, which will give you a feel for how much more time it takes to recite the Qur'an formally than it does to do a simple recitation.

To the extent that you are able, try during prayer to chant the Qur'an melodically (adhering to the rules of *tajwīd*) rather than simply reciting it. Your chanting of the text will give you a clearer sense of individual responsibility towards it, a deeper reverence, awe and respect, and a concern to duplicate with absolute fidelity the words of God Almighty as they were conveyed by the angel Gabriel.

16

The New Language of the Qur'an

Something that may help you to develop, deepen and improve your recitation of the Qur'an is the realisation that when you recite the Qur'an, you are not dealing with ordinary, traditional, human language. What most moved the early Muslims when they heard the Qur'an on the lips of their Prophet for the first time was not the beauty of its language; nor was it its fine rhetorical style, its eloquence, its meanings, its clarity, its precision or its rhythm. Rather, what shook them to the core was the simultaneous presence of all these features side by side with something far greater and more remarkable, something which, despite their linguistic prowess and expertise and their confidence and pride in their poetry, literature and eloquence, they had never observed in their language before. This 'something' was the newness and uniqueness of the language being used, which differed qualitatively from that of any Arab they had ever encountered before, including the Messenger of God himself.

Prior to Muhammad's call to prophethood, his fellow Arabs had been familiar with the language he customarily used, and which had been essentially no different than their own. Hence, it must have been an earthshaking event when, one morning, they woke up to find him addressing them in a language that differed entirely from both his accustomed form of linguistic expression, and theirs. It was distinct with respect to its particles, its vocabulary, its expressions, its idioms, its connectors, its images, and its rhetorical features. But at the same time – and herein lies the miraculous, unsettling aspect of it – the language he was now using was still pure, unadulterated Arabic founded upon the established rules of the language with which they were so familiar. This was the case despite all the additions that had been introduced, the new conventions that now enriched it, and the unlimited horizons it had opened up for innovation and development.

What they were faced with was an extraordinary combination of the basic rules of Arabic, on which the new language rested and which it had preserved fully intact, and a departure from the traditional, familiar conventions of terminology and grammar. This unprecedented mix, with its distinctiveness, newness and uniqueness, is sufficiently intense and out of the ordinary to shake us up, to excite us, and to inspire an attitude of humble reverence as we repeat it in our prayers. And for this very reason, the chapters of this Divinely inspired book bear a new, unique name – *sūrah*, literally, 'wall' or 'fence' – which signals their impenetrability by any creature and the impossibility of their being mimicked or forged.

The units, or verses, into which the *sūrahs* of the Qur'an are divided also bear a distinctive name – *Āyah*, or 'sign/miracle'

– which affirms the miraculous nature of this linguistic phenomenon and the impossibility of forging it, imitating it, or penetrating its mystery for all time to come.[23]

17

Open Language and 'Fertile Spaces'

We frequently encounter words and phrases that we are so accustomed to hearing or repeating that we pass over them without a second thought. We treat them as though they were entirely ordinary even though if we stripped our memories of the effects of habit or familiarity we would see them to be otherwise. Of relevance here is the following Hadith: 'When bowing and prostrating, the Prophet (pbuh) used to say, "*Subbūḥun quddūs rabbu al-malā'ikati wa al-rūḥ*" (Most Deemed far above, Most Holy One, [You are] the Master of the angels and of the spirit).'[24]

Like the term *subḥāna*, virtually always used before the name of God in the sense of 'God be deemed far above', the term *subbūḥ* was only introduced into the Arabic language with the advent of Islam. Both these terms are open-ended in nature in the sense that they leave a 'blank space' for us to fill in with our own conceptualisations or imaginations as they relate to traits of the Divine perfection. In this respect, such terms resemble the phrase *Allāhu Akbar*.

With its *fu'lān* morphological pattern, the term *subḥān* is an unusual verbal noun. Like the term *subbūḥ*, it has the effect of exalting the person being spoken of, of declaring this individual to be 'above' a certain quality or action. Hence, when we say, *subḥāna rabbiya*, we are saying, in effect, 'I hold my Lord to be blameless or devoid of...' (*unazzihu rabbī 'an...)*. The question then arises, 'Of what quality or action do I hold my Lord to be blameless or devoid?' The answer to this question is not mentioned in the formulas of praise uttered during the bow and prostration of the Salah. Instead they are left open, linguistically incomplete, and followed by a semantic space that we are free to fill with whatever we choose. In this respect, these two phrases are like the open-ended *Allāhu Akbar,* as though we were to say, for example, *subḥāna rabbiya al-a'lā, subḥāna rabbiya al-'aẓīm*, that is, 'My Lord, the Highly Exalted, is far above, My Lord, the Almighty, is far above...', who is far above imperfection, shame, weariness, injustice, error, weakness, slumber, illness, etc.

The Salah contains numerous phrases that are grammatically and semantically incomplete and which, for this reason, are open to a multitude of possibilities. Surprisingly, however, they occur side by side with phrases that are complete, but which are open-ended for other reasons. This latter type of phrase occurs in abundance in the *Fātiḥah*, for example, as well as in the formulaic greetings and supplications that form part of the Salah.

In the course of every pair of *rak'ahs* of the Salah, we utter no fewer than thirty-three expressions that are linguistically incomplete. What this means is that we have thirty-three 'open spaces' which we can fill with our imaginations, and which allow us sufficient time to take in their meanings and make them present to our minds. This number does not include the *Fātiḥah*, the greetings and supplications uttered to and on behalf of the Prophet and others. Nor does it include other verses or traditional supplications or litanies that might form part of our prayer. The three-thirty open-ended expressions that form a part of every Salah are detailed as follows:

1) Eleven utterances of *Allāhu Akbar* ('God is greater...': greater than what?)
2) Two utterances of *sami'a Allāhu li man ḥamidah* ('God hears those who praise Him': who praise Him for what?)
3) Two utterances of *rabbanā wa laka al-ḥamd* ('And to You, O Lord, belongs all praise': praise for what?)
4) Six (2 bows x 3) utterances of *subḥāna rabbiya al'āẓīm* ('My Lord, the Almighty, is far above': far above what?), and
5) Twelve (4 prostrations x 3) *subḥāna rabbiya al-a'lā* ('My Lord the Most Highly Exalted is far above': far above what?)

The frequency with which such open-ended, linguistically incomplete phrases occur points to the importance of the imaginative element for making the best use of the diversity that marks Salah, for maintaining the greatest degree of humble reverence, for cultivating understanding and awareness of what one is saying as a worshipper and, hence, making genuine contact with God.

However, it is important to distinguish here between what we are terming an 'open-ended but linguistically complete expression', and an 'open-ended and linguistically incomplete expression'. Every linguistically incomplete expression is also an open-ended expression; however, not all open-ended expressions are linguistically incomplete.

The expressions, *subḥāna rabbī* ('My Lord is far above'), *sami'a Allāhu li man ḥamidah* ('God hears those who praise/ thank Him'), and *rabbanā wa laka al-ḥamd* ('And to You, O Lord, belongs all praise/thanks'), for example, are linguistically incomplete; as a result, they are followed by a kind of 'horizontal space' that can be filled in various different ways. As for the open-ended terms or expressions which we find in the *Fātiḥah*, by contrast, they are complete both linguistically and grammatically, and for this reason they need no horizontal addition; nevertheless, they are subject to more than one interpretation. Given these various possible interpretations, they are open-ended expressions. However, the additions to which they are open are 'vertical' in the sense that they add semantic depth despite the phrase's grammatical completeness. This kind of multi-layered phrase or term might be likened to a building with several storeys or levels, each of which has its own distinctive content, flavour and hue.

18

THE ROLE OF THE *FĀTIḤAH*

Have you ever stopped to think about the fact that the *Fātiḥah* is not simply the opening *sūrah* or chapter of the Qur'an, but is also the opening to Salah? In fact, the *Fātiḥah* could be said to be prayer itself. In the words of God Almighty communicated through the Prophet, 'I have divided prayer (that is, the *Fātiḥah*) between Myself and My servant.'[25]

And have you ever thought of this prayer as a kind of sacred covenant between two parties: the worshipper (Party 2), and the One Worshipped (Party 1)? According to this covenant, Party 2 pledges the following to Party 1: continuous praise and thanksgiving (*al-ḥamdu lillāhi*, 'All praise is due to God alone'), recognition of His lordship and sovereignty (*rabbi al-'ālamīn* , 'the Sustainer of all the worlds'), recognition of His constant mercy (*al-Raḥmān al-Raḥīm*, 'the most Gracious, the Dispenser of Grace, now and for all time'), and of His kingly rule and absolute governance of the universe on the Day of Resurrection (*Māliki yawm al-dīn*, 'Lord of the Day of Judgment'); as well as obedient servanthood and surrender to Him and recognition of His oneness (*iyyāka na'budu*, 'You alone do we worship'). In return, Party 1 promises Party 2 to come to his aid in all his affairs (*iyyāka nasta'īn*, 'To You alone do we turn for aid'), to guide him in this earthly realm along the straight path (*al-ṣirāṭ al-mustaqīm*) to which He guides the beloved servants upon whom His blessing lies, and to spare them the fate of those who have earned His displeasure (*al-maghḍūbi 'alayhim*, 'those who have been condemned'), as well as those who have gone astray (*al-ḍāllīn*) by no longer worshipping Him in His true oneness.

While reciting the *Fātiḥah*, have you thought about the fact that it is not ordinary human speech: that it differs not only from the Arabic used in day-to-day lives, but even, based on all the narratives that have come down to us, from that used by the Prophet himself in his day?

What would you say if I told you that the *Fātiḥah*, which consists of twenty-nine words in the original Arabic, contains no fewer than fifty-eight linguistic phenomena with which the Arabs of the Prophet's day had been unfamiliar prior to the revelation of the Qur'an? These new linguistic features were foreign even to the everyday language of the Messenger of God, the only exceptions being places in which he was quoting from the Qur'an itself.[26]

Try to remember all this when you recite the *Fātiḥah* in prayer. And in order to bring its meanings still closer to your heart and digest the spirit of its words, try to imagine that you yourself are the one bringing forth the words out of your own mind. Imagine that you are the person who formulated it, yet without forgetting that it is God's inimitable, incomparable self-expression. If you can do this, you will begin to feel the words welling up from within you, and your heart beating to their rhythm. You will feel that you are uttering words you truly mean and that reflect what you truly believe rather than simply parroting words that were spoken by someone else, that you do not really understand, and that elicit no inward response on your part.

If you pass this test, you will have taken your first step down the path towards sensing the value of every word of this distinctive *sūrah*, experiencing the majesty of every phrase, and comprehending the wondrous meanings it conveys.

Always remember that this *sūrah* of the Qur'an has special importance. No matter what other *surahs* or passages you happen to recite in your prayer, none of them could take the place of the *Fātiḥah*. Even if you recited every other *sūrah* of the entire Qur'an in a single prayer, but failed to recite the *Fātiḥah*, it would be as though you had not prayed. You may have been given credit for your recitation, but not for your prayer. As the Prophet once said, 'No prayer shall be attributed to someone who did not recite the Holy Book's opening *sūrah* (that is, the *Fātiḥah*).'

> In the name of God, the Immanently Merciful, the ever-Merciful (*bismillāhi al-raḥmāni al-raḥīm*):[27]

The *basmalah* – the phrase, *bismillāh al-raḥmān al-raḥīm* – is one of the most beautiful verses in the Qur'an, if not the most beautiful of all. However, repetition, habit and familiarity have obscured its beauty from us. We repeat it as though it were just a polite phrase like 'thank you', 'pardon me', and 'goodbye'. But we might ask ourselves: Why did the Lord of the Worlds choose this as the first *āyah* we repeat in the Salah? Why is it the phrase with which the Qur'an opens? Why does it introduce all but one of the *sūrahs* of the Qur'an? And why is it an integral part of the *Fātiḥah*?

The fact that we utter the phrase, *bismillāh al-raḥmān al-raḥīm*, 'In the name of God, the Most Gracious, the Dispenser of Grace, now and for all time' as we begin to pray, as we begin reciting the Qur'an, and at the beginning of nearly every one of its *sūrahs*, not to mention the fact that we are accustomed to uttering it whenever we commence some action in our day-to-day lives, has given us the illusion that it means nothing more than the beginning of a new task. In fact, Arab grammarians have fallen prey to the same illusion. Consequently, they have made little effort to identify the implied verb or the actual event with which they associate the preposition (Arabic, bi, or English, 'in') and the genitive case (*majrūr*) that follows it (the Arabic word for 'name', ism, is in the genitive case because it follows a preposition). Some grammarians hold that the implied action or event is 'I begin', the full meaning of the phrase being, 'In the name of God I begin' (*bismillāhi abda'u*). In so saying, they may have solved a grammatical conundrum; however, they have done nothing to elucidate the true meaning of the phrase.

The fact that the *basmalah* is used so frequently to introduce an action or a sacred text has given rise to the illusion that, in essence, it is merely this – a preface to something else. However, the most important message of the *basmalah* is that any Qur'anic statement that follows it, be it a command or a prohibition, a promise or a threat, a description or a report, an exhortation or a reminder, will be communicated on God's behalf, and by His authority.

Human beings are God's vicegerents or representatives on Earth (cf. *al-Baqarah* 2:30). So, as they prepare to recite the words of the One who has assigned them responsibility for the earth, and as they strive to reproduce these words in the form in which they were first revealed, they should remember, and remind those who hear them, that they are reciting them on God's behalf, by His authority, and in their capacity as His proxies on Earth.

When a judge commences a verdict with the words, 'In the name of the people,' he is issuing the verdict on the people's behalf and in his capacity as their representative, or as one they have assigned to carry out a particular task, since he derives his authority from them and his decisions are made in accordance with their laws. Similarly, when we begin our recitation of the *Fātiḥah* with the words, 'In the name of God, the Gracious, the Dispenser of Grace, now and for all time,' this serves as a reminder to us that whatever heaven-sent teachings or instructions we convey, we will be conveying by God's power and authority. If, with the grammarians, we hold that the *basmalah* implies a prior, but unstated verb phrase such as 'I begin...' (such that the entire statement is 'In the name of God I begin,' or 'I begin in the name of God'), we spare ourselves the trouble of searching and exploring. At the same time, we close off a horizon and lose sight of the phrase's most important and fundamental meaning.

When I begin the Salah with the *basmalah*, this should serve as a reminder to me that what I am about to engage in is more than a series of unthinking movements or the repetition of memorised lines that have no connection with the rest of my being. Rather, it is a genuine act of communication with God in which I keep the covenant between us and affirm my desire to be His faithful steward and proxy on Earth.

Similarly, when I feature the *basmalah* on the first page of this book, it acts as a reminder to me from the Lord of the Worlds, and as an affirmation by me to Him, that everything in it from beginning to end will be consistent with the covenant between us. It means that in every word it contains start to finish I seek His pleasure, I abide by His commands, I respect the limits He has set, and I adhere to the conditions He has laid down for the legitimate use of the earthly authority invested in me. The *basmalah* is like a document affirming that you are nothing but a proxy for God in this earthly sphere. There is no rule or authority but God's. There is no wealth or property but that it belongs to God. There is no food or drink but that God is its Source. We human beings were only sent down from the heavenly realm to this tiny fiefdom known as 'Planet Earth' - which is undoubtedly only one among billions and billions of other fiefdoms, large and small, scattered throughout this vast Universe - to manage its affairs on behalf of its Proprietor, and to carry out the provisions of the contract between us that will soon come to an end. So, then, are we prepared for our imminent departure? Have we prepared ourselves to appear before the Proprietor with the accounts ledgers in our hands?

However, the story of the *basmalah* does not end here. This 'franchise' or contract of representation might have ended with the words 'in the name of God' (*bismillāh*). Instead, however, God Almighty has linked it to an addendum that serves as an inseparable part of it, namely the words, 'the Most Gracious, the Dispenser of Grace, now and for all time' (*al-Raḥmān al-Raḥīm*). The consistent conjunction of the two words *al-Raḥmān* and *al-Raḥīm*, both of which are derived from a single root, in the *basmalah* (the 'contract of representation' between us and God), and the *basmalah's* position at the beginning of the two most important means of communication between Muslims and their Lord - Salah and the Qur'an - convey several messages.

First: Because, as we are told in a Divine saying conveyed through the Prophet, God's mercy precedes His wrath, He has chosen to have us commence our prayers with this particular dual appellation. This choice on God's part is made clear through the fact that no fewer than 113 out of the Qur'an's 114 chapters begin with the *basmalah*, and this despite the fact that the two Divine names it contains are derived from the same root. Note that there is no variety in the pairs of Divine names used to introduce the various *sūrahs* of the Qur'an; in other words, the *basmalah* is never replaced by some other pair of Divine names/attributes. We do not find, for example, a *sūrah* introduced by a pair of Divine names that would balance mercy with rigour, and this despite the fact that such pairings occur frequently in the Qur'an, and despite the availability of pairings that show other contrasting etymologies, as in the phrase describing God as 'Almighty, a Dispenser of Grace, now and for all time' (*al-Shu'arā* 26:9), or 'Almighty, Truly Forgiving' (*al-Mulk* 67:2).

Second: Because the dual attributes of *al-Raḥmān* and *al-Raḥīm* enjoy such importance, being a fundamental part of the Salah and a preface to any Qur'anic recitation you might do, they thus constitute a pillar of Islam's doctrinal teaching. Hence, if you are worthy to be God's proxy on Earth, this pillar of Islamic teaching must be evident in your behaviour and attitudes.

Third: Because you have been appointed God's steward on Earth, God being 'the Most Gracious, Most Merciful, now and for all time', this requires you, in keeping with these two descriptions chosen by the Divine Himself, to be the best steward possible. In view of the Qur'an's repeated, insistent use of these two descriptors for God, you must rise consistently to the challenge you have been given by being the embodiment of grace and compassion. If you are a Muslim, then the world should see – in the kindness of your features, the warmth of your smile, the gentility of your treatment of others both near and far, your love for and patience with friend and foe alike – the true meaning of grace and compassion, readiness to forgive, and the willingness to embrace others.

So, you might ask yourself: Is this the image of Islam that is reflected in my life today?

> *Al-Raḥmān al-Raḥīm*: 'The Most Gracious, Most Merciful, Now and for All Time.'

Although the terms *al-Raḥmān* and *al-Raḥīm* are both based on the trilateral root *r-ḥ-m*, from which we derive the word for mercy or compassion (*raḥmah*), they nevertheless follow two distinct morphological patterns: *fa'lān* and *fa'īl*. Consequently, each of them has its own distinctive character and personality. The *fa'lān* pattern of adjective tends to bear a sense of immediacy and to be used to speak about something happening now, at this moment. It is illustrated in the Arabic adjectives *'aṭshān*, 'thirsty'; *ghaḍbān*, 'angry'; *sahrān*, 'wakeful, watchful'; and *farhān*, 'joyful', each of which describes a present condition or state. Someone we describe as *'aṭshān* is thirsty now, but may not remain thirsty for long. Similarly, someone we describe as *ghaḍbān*, or angry, will not necessarily go on being angry. Hence, *al-Raḥmān*, variously translated as 'Most Gracious', 'Most Merciful' and 'Most Compassionate', is the One whose grace, mercy and compassion are descending upon you from on high 'now', that is, at the moment at which you utter the word *al-Raḥmān*. As such, the term *al-Raḥmān* conveys a sense of dynamic immediacy, as though spiritual power was extending vertically from Heaven to Earth. With the use of this attribute we feel Divine mercy and compassion moving towards us, descending freshly upon us, bringing immediate refreshment from on high. So, when you utter this word, make a point of feeling mercy descend like a waterfall that engulfs you, washing you from head to toe in Almighty God's overflowing compassion.

As for the term *al-Raḥīm*, which follows the morphological pattern *fa'īl*, it tends to convey a sense of permanence and continuity over time. Hence, a generous person (*karīm*) is generous by nature; generosity is an abiding feature of this person's character. Similarly, a miserly person (*bakhīl*) is miserly by nature, and thus demonstrates this quality consistently over time, while the vulgar, ill-mannered individual (*waḍī'*) is ill-mannered not only in specific situations, but wherever he finds himself. Hence, when we speak of God as *al-Raḥīm*, we are saying that He is the One whose mercy encompasses us at all times, and that just as God was merciful and compassionate in the past, so also is God merciful and compassionate in the present, and will be so in the future. Mercy and compassion are abiding, permanent features of God's character, who has been gracious, merciful and compassionate for all eternity and will continue to be so for all eternity. Hence, we might say that with its extended, 'horizontal' dimension, the descriptor *al-Raḥīm* complements the word *al-Raḥmān* with its immediate, 'vertical' dimension.[28]

The appropriateness of the distinction I have drawn between these two Divine attributes and their defining dimensions is confirmed by the way in which the Messenger himself used to recite them.

> Anas was once asked, 'How the Messenger of God (pbuh) used to recite?' And he replied, 'He would recite by drawing out the words (*kānat qirā'atuhu maddan*).' Then [in demonstration of the Prophet's manner of

> recitation], he recited the phrase *bismillāh al-Raḥmān al-Raḥīm*, saying, 'He would prolong the phrase *bismillāh*, "in the name of God". And he would do the same with the name *al-Raḥmān*, and with the name *al-Raḥīm*.'[29]

The act of drawing out the pronunciation of the phrase *al-Raḥmān*, as well as the phrase *al-Raḥīm*, despite the fact that neither of these words contains any of the features that, based on the rules of *tajwīd*, would require such prolongation, lends each of these two phrases a kind of autonomy and a distinctiveness of its own. By increasing the temporal distance between one phrase and the next, this manner of recitation acts to separate the first descriptor from the one that follows it. Moreover, separation means autonomy and uniqueness in both sense and orientation.

19

Red Key No. 2: 'You alone do we worship, and unto You alone do we turn for aid'

Iyyāka naʿbudu wa iyyāka nastaʿīn

Picture a man who has been wronged in some way and who has come to a government office in the hope of claiming his rights. He walks in to see some government employee and presents his demands. The employee, for his part, tells the man to fill out a certain form, put it in a stamped envelope and send it to the relevant government agency so that his case can go through the proper channels. And once the official authorised to evaluate the petition makes a decision on his case, the man will have no choice but to accept the outcome whether it is right or wrong, fair or unfair. Then compare this man's situation to that of another, more fortunate, individual who is a close personal acquaintance of the aforementioned official, who has the final say on what becomes of every petition submitted to the agency and who, moreover, is a just, discerning man of impeccable integrity who would never wrong a soul.

Even though nothing and no one can be properly compared to God Almighty, who is above and beyond all categories of human thought, the statement, 'To You alone we turn for aid' nevertheless reflects a situation that bears some resemblance to the one I have just described. When dealing with God Almighty Himself, your complaint need not be heard by some petty employee, and you are not required to submit a formal petition through 'proper channels'. Instead, you are allowed - in fact, you are commanded - to address 'the Official in charge' directly, and to ask Him for whatever you need. Not only that, but this 'Official' gives you the formulation He wants you to use in making your request. Placing on your lips the attributes with which He has described Himself in the opening verses of the *Fātiḥah*, He gives you the opportunity to affirm that you are His servant and that He is your Lord and your God, the One responsible for you and for meeting all your needs ('You alone do we worship'). The Messenger of God once said:

> God Almighty tells us, 'I have divided prayer - that is, the *Fātiḥah* - equally between Myself and My servant. Half of it is for Me, and half of it is for my servant. Moreover, My servant will receive whatever he/she asks. When the servant says, "All praise is due to God alone, Sustainer of all the worlds" (*al-ḥamdu lillāhi rabbi al-'ālamīn*), I will say, "My servant has praised Me." When My servant says, "the Most Gracious, Most Merciful, now and for all time" (*al-Raḥmān al-Raḥīm*), I will say, "My servant has extolled Me." When My servant describes Me as "Lord of the Day of Judgment" (*Maliki yawmi al-dīn*), I will say, "My servant has glorified Me." If My servant says, "You alone do we worship, and

> unto You alone do we turn for aid" (*iyyāka na'budu wa iyyāka nasta'īn*), I will say, "This [verse] is divided between Me and My servant." Moreover, My servant shall receive whatever he/she asks. When My servant says, "Guide us the straight way" (*ihdinā al-ṣirāṭa al-mustaqīm*), "the way of those upon whom You have bestowed Your blessings, not of those who have been condemned by You, nor of those that go astray" (*ṣirāṭa al-ladhīna an'amta 'alayhim ghayri al-maghḍūbi 'alayhim wa lā al-ḍāllīn*), I will say, "This is for My servant, and My servant will receive whatever he/she has asked".'[30]

We are now at the central point of the verse which is, in turn, at the central point of the *Fātiḥah*. This midpoint marks the end of the first section, which is characterised by the worshipper's lifting of affirmation, praise and adoration to God ('You alone do we worship'), and the beginning of the second section, which is characterised by supplication and entreaty in which the worshipper makes requests of God ('Unto You alone do we turn for aid').

When we reach this transition point, we may sense the remarkable distinctiveness of the two 'stations' that are joined by this single verse, or *āyah*. As such, we may feel the need to pause in our recitation at the first half of the verse ('You alone do we worship') before going on to the second half ('Unto You alone do we turn for aid'). And in fact, 'Ali ibn Abī Ṭālib is reported to have recited the phrase 'we worship' (*na'budu*) in such a way that 'the letter *dāl* is drawn out to the point where it generates the "u" sound of the following letter *wāw*.'[31] This way of pronouncing the phrase *na'budu* serves to reveal and emphasise the distinctive 'personalities' of the two halves of the *Fātiḥah* between which it is situated.

As you utter these two phrases in your prayer, have you ever sensed that, although they appear in a single verse, they represent two disparate attitudes or positions, and that the tone you adopt in the first part of the verse ('You alone do we worship') should be different from the tone you use in the second ('Unto You alone do we turn for aid')? If so, this is only fitting, since you are crossing over from the section that pertains to Party 1 of the contract (God Almighty) to the section that pertains to Party 2 (the worshipper).

As you recite the words, 'You alone do we worship,' your voice should be marked by a tone of reverence, awe and submission in the face of the One who holds your life and destiny in His hands. And when you come to the phrase, 'Unto You alone do we turn for aid,' your tone should be one of earnest pleading, entreaty, supplication and hope as you anticipate the outpouring of Divine mercy and succour. And how could it be otherwise when you know that you are being heard by the Almighty One who, if He be against you, no one can deliver you and who, if He be for you, no one can stand against you?

It is in relation to this verse that the most trustworthy of Promisers has made His adoring servant the most wonderful of promises, saying, 'And My servant will receive whatever he/she has asked.' So, when you say, 'Unto You alone do we turn for aid,' do so in full confidence that the aid you seek is truly yours. Do so with the confidence of the worshipper who, when he went one scorching, parched day to offer the prayer for rain with a group of fellow believers, came back carrying an umbrella under his arm.

Guide us the straight way

Now that the doors of praise have been opened to you and you have offered God heartfelt thanks; now that the doors of mercy have been opened and you have entered them gladly and humbly; now that you have been given the opportunity to ask and you have requested fully, the Lord of the Worlds has placed in your mouth the greatest request anyone could make in this life: the request to be guided to the straight path. Is there anything we fear more than to miss our way to this path?

Imagine being as wealthy, intelligent, healthy and happy as anyone could possibly be, yet without having been graced with true guidance and faith in God's oneness. Of what use would your worldly happiness be if you were deprived of happiness in the life to come? What is a hundred years, a thousand years, a hundred thousand years, or even a million years of life in this world compared with a single moment in the realm of eternity, be it in bliss or in torment? As we read in the Qur'an, 'But as for those who are bent on denying the truth, their [good] deeds are like a mirage in the desert, which the thirsty supposes to be water - until, when he approaches it, he finds that it was nothing: instead, he finds God there, and [that] He will pay him his account in full - for God is swift in reckoning!' (*al-Nūr* 24:39). The following tradition, declared authentic by al-Albānī and narrated by Ibn Mājah on the authority of Anas Ibn Mālik, affirms the same truth:

> On the Day of Resurrection, one of the unbelievers who had been most richly blessed in this world will be brought forth. It will then be said, 'Dip him a single time into the Fire.' After being dipped into the Fire,

> he will be asked, 'Have you ever known blessedness, O so-and-so?' 'No, never!' he will reply. Then one of the believers who had suffered the most severely in this world will be brought forth, and it will be said, 'Dip him a single time into the river of Paradise.' After being dipped into the river of Paradise, the believer will be asked, 'Have you ever suffered harm or tribulation, O so-and-so?' And he will reply, 'No, never!'

The pleasure we experience when we pray, 'Unto You alone do we turn for aid,' is different from the pleasure we feel when, immediately after this, we plead, 'Guide us the straight way.' The first phrase is usually a request for worldly succour or sustenance, while the second is generally a request relating to the world to come. This does not preclude its being a prayer for guidance in this world as well, of course. The phrase, 'the straight way' is semantically open. For in addition to referring to Divine guidance and belief in God's oneness, it can also refer to wisdom, discretion, and the ability to form well-founded opinions on things. And could there be a worldly blessing greater than the ability to think soundly about the affairs of one's life, and to help others to do the same?

The open quality that characterises the term 'way' (*ṣirāṭ*) applies to other terms throughout the *Fātiḥah* as well. Who, for example, are 'those upon whom Thou hast bestowed Your blessings' (*alladhīna an'amta 'alayhim),* 'those who have been condemned' (*al-maghḍūbi 'alayhim*), and 'those who go astray' (*al-ḍāllīn*) spoken of at the end of the *Fātiḥah*?

Each of the aforementioned phrases is linguistically complete. As such, none of them is followed by a 'virtual empty space' that invites us to fill it in with our imaginations. However, if we compare them with other expressions used in everyday human speech, their open quality becomes apparent.

In order to better grasp the difference between open-ended and closed language, let us read the passage again, substituting the 'open' Qur'anic phrases with alternative, 'closed' phrases. The passage now reads, 'Guide us on the straight way, the way of the "A" people, not the way of the "B" nor the way of the "C" people.' This alternative, 'closed' reading highlights, by way of contrast, the richness of the Qur'anic language, which allows us to interpret the phrase 'those upon whom You have bestowed Your blessings' (*alladhīna an'amta 'alayhim*) as applying to every person who has been blessed with grace in any form; it allows us to understand the words 'those who have been condemned' (*al-maghḍūbi 'alayhim*) as referring to anyone with whom God is displeased, and to construe the phrase 'those who go astray' (*al-ḍāllīn*) as a reference to everyone who has lost his or her way to the truth. This openness does not cancel out or preclude the interpretation offered by the Prophet; yet neither does it 'close off' the three expressions such that each of them refers to one specific group only and to no other.

When we read or recite the prayer, 'guide us (on) the straight way,' it is important to remember that this and numerous other phrases repeated in the Salah have come down to us in an 'open' form for some reason in the Divine wisdom. It is because of these phrases' open quality that, if we choose, we can think of them as including every creature on Earth, just as, if we choose, we can narrow them to the point where they hardly include even ourselves. It bears noting that this prayer is not in the singular form ('Guide me...'). Rather, it is in the plural form ('Guide us...'). With this in mind, try allowing this prayer to embrace everyone around you, from children and other family members, to neighbours and acquaintances, to the entire world, including friend and foe alike, Muslim and non-Muslim. How could there be anything more marvellous than to ask God to pour out His blessings upon your friends, your enemies and all of humanity without exception; for Him to guide them in His grace to the truth, to justice, and to 'the straight way'? Indeed, did not our Prophet pray to God to empower Islam by one of the two (non-Muslim) 'Umars? The prayer which was later to gift Islam with the great caliph 'Umar ibn al-Khaṭṭāb!

Remember that by shifting from the exclusive 'I' to the inclusive 'we', we break down the barriers of hatred and bitterness between ourselves and others, whoever they happen to be. And in so doing, we declare our determination to respond with love and tolerance towards those who glorify hatred, and who teach their children that in order to be Muslims, they have to hate and resent others. So, remember this golden rule: You are a Muslim; therefore, you are loving and accepting:

> Hold to forgiveness, enjoin the good and turn away from the ignorant. (*al-A'rāf* 7:199)

> ...whoever pardons [his foe] and makes peace, his reward rests with God. (*al-Shūrā* 42:40)

> ...But if you pardon [their faults] and forbear, and forgive – then, behold, God will be Much-Forgiving, a Dispenser of Grace. (*al-Taghābun* 64:14)

Vowel Elongation (Madd) in the Fātiḥah

Prolongation of a vowel sound, referred to in Arabic as *madd*, amounts to a brief pause in speech. Hence, it gives the word or phrase in which the vowel sound occurs its own personality and a greater degree of autonomy, since the temporal lag involved allows time to reflect on and digest the meaning of the word or expression in which the *madd* took place.

We must distinguish here between complete pauses in recitation and madd, which is a special kind of pause or 'semi-pause'. The Messenger of God would come to a complete halt in his recitation before and after the *Fātiḥah*. He would do the same between verses, or *āyahs*, which provided a 'fertile space' between one verse and the next. As for the pauses, or, rather, semi-pauses within verses that result from *madd*, they mark our recitation with greater reverence, and enhance our ability to bring the text's meanings consciously to mind and take in what we are reciting. As for the pauses between verses, they give us time not only to reflect on the preceding verse, but to anticipate the verse that will follow. Among the twenty-nine words that make up the *Fātiḥah*, I have counted up no fewer than twenty-two cases of *madd*. These are in addition to the natural pauses between verses, of which there are seven. Hence, the frequency of pauses in the *Fātiḥah* is far higher than what one encounters in day-to-day conversation and writings; nor do you encounter it in other chapters of the Qur'an.

The successive cases of madd in the *Fātiḥah* represent a departure from the rules of *tajwīd* overall. In fact, the *Fātiḥah* is almost entirely devoid of the linguistic phenomena to which the rules of *tajwīd* apply. This constitutes still another unique feature of the *Fātiḥah* that can help us to immerse ourselves in reflection, surrender and reverence for the One in whose presence we stand.

If, for example, we tally the instances of *madd* in *al-Kawthar* (*Sūrah* No. 108) and *al-Ikhlāṣ*| (*Sūrah* No. 112), two of the shortest chapters of the Qur'an, we find that in al-Kawthar, there are three cases of *madd* out of a total of ten words (in the words *innā, a'ṭaynāk, and shāni'aka*), whereas in *al-Ikhlāṣ*|, there are only four cases of *madd* (in the terms Allāh, Allāh, *yūlad* and *lahu*) out of a total of fifteen words.

As we conclude this particular discussion, allow me to say again that whatever thoughts, analyses and suggestions I offer here remain no more than products of my human mind. As such, they are subject to criticism and refutation. If evidence shows that my proposals or analyses are invalid, I will be the first to acknowledge the authority of the sacred text, and to support the evidence over my own hypotheses. As a Muslim, how could I do otherwise?

20

The Centrality of Bowing and Prostration

The first time I went on the Hajj at the age of forty, I felt like an awkward little boy as I was walking, circumambulating the Ka'bah. As I did the rounds of the Ka'bah wrapped in a couple of simple pieces of white cloth, I could hear Satan whispering, 'What if your university students (and among them were Muslims and non-Muslims) saw you looking like this? They would say, "What's happened to our professor? He usually looks so imposing and dignified!"' Fortunately, it was not long before a spirit of faith won out, reminding me of who I am. 'I am a Muslim, which means that I live in a state of surrender and obedience. I am nothing but a meek, humble servant. In other words, I am nothing before the Almighty, All-Powerful, Majestic One who owns the heavens and the earth, who gives life and deals death.'

And from then on, whenever I submitted myself humbly to God in acts of worship, I would find these same refreshing spiritual breezes blowing over me. I could feel them every time I bowed, and every time I praised Him and declared His perfection and freedom from all fault, weakness, injustice, imperfection, weariness and inattention. I would feel them as I rose from the bowing position, uttering the words, *samiʿa Allāhu li man ḥamidah* ('God hears those who praise Him'), then responding, *rabbanā wa laka al-ḥamd* ('To You, O Lord, all praise is due') for creating me, guiding me aright, and giving me all the blessings I enjoy. I would feel them still as I prostrated and praised Him again with the words *subḥāna rabbiya al-aʿlā* ('My most exalted Lord is far above') declaring Him free of all manner of imperfection. With my head in the lowest possible position in God's presence, I felt as close to Heaven as I could possibly be.

> I once encountered Thawbān, a freed slave of the Messenger of God (pbuh), and I said to him, 'Tell me something that, if I do it, will ensure that God ushers me into Paradise.'[32] But he made no reply. I asked the question again, and he still said nothing in response. When I asked him the third time, he said, 'I posed this same question to the Messenger of God, and he said, "Prostrate yourself often before God. For every prostration you perform, God will raise you up by a degree and absolve you of one of your sins."'[33]

Did you know that some people, even as they worship God, are committing theft? They do so between one bow and the next, one prostration and the next. And, stranger still, these people are not stealing from others, but from themselves!

> Before the Divinely ordained punishments for drinking, adultery and theft had been revealed, [the Prophet once asked some of his followers], 'What do

> you think of those who drink, commit adultery and steal?' 'God and His Prophet can judge them best,' they replied. 'They are abominations,' he told them, 'and there are punishments prescribed for them. But the worst kind of thief is one who robs his own prayer.' 'And how could someone rob of his own prayer?' they asked. 'By not properly performing his bows and prostrations.'[34]

What the Prophet said makes perfect sense, of course. After all, the Salah came to us as a gift from God, as 'a sacred duty linked to particular times [of day]' (*al-Nisā'* 4:103) by means of which spiritual sums are deposited daily in our other-worldly accounts. For many, however, Salah has become 'busy work', and a waste of time. For people who have come to see Salah not as a right, but as a duty, it amounts to nothing but a set of hurried movements to be finished with as quickly as possible.

> [The Prophet once said], 'Salah consists of three equal parts. The first part consists in achieving and maintaining ritual purity. The second part consists in bowing. And the third part consists in prostration. If one gives Salah its due, it will be accepted from him, as will all of his other good works. But if one's Salah is not accepted by God, then all of his other good works will be rejected as well.'[35]

Just think: If bowing is counted as one-third of one's prayer, if prostrating is counted as another third, and if ritual purity is counted as the final third, what does the everything else amount to? Note that bowing and prostrating are the only two movements that are required of us in Salah. We begin the prayer standing still and we end it in a seated position. Apart from these two still positions, the only movements involved in the prayer are bowing and prostration.

Another point worth noting is that the Messenger of God focuses on joining each of these two movements with an open-ended expression followed by moments of quiet reflection. When we utter the phrase, *Allāhu Akbar*, 'God is greater...', its open-ended nature requires us to follow it with a time of silent reflection: God is greater...than what? We utter the words, *sami'a Allāhu li man ḥamidah*, 'God hears those who praise/thank Him,' followed by, *rabbanā wa laka al-ḥamd*, 'To You, O Lord, all praise/thanks are due,' which is to be followed by still more silent reflection: Praise/thanks is due for what? Similarly, after uttering the phrases, *subḥāna rabbiya al-'aẓīm*, 'my Lord the Almighty is far above,' and *subḥāna rabbiya al-a'lā*, 'My Lord the highly exalted is far above,' we are to pause and ask ourselves: Over what is He highly exalted?

It is on this basis that bowing and prostrating are counted as two-thirds of the Salah. When you say the words, *subḥāna rabbiya al-'aẓīm (when bowing) or subḥāna rabbiya al-a'lā* (when prostrating), bring to mind something that will help you to appreciate God's greatness and majesty. In this way you can turn your words of praise, and indeed, your entire prayer, from a mere habit into genuine worship.

If the words, *Allāhu Akbar* are your chance to learn greater patience and perseverance, this will strengthen you to cope with the difficulties and trials you face in life.

If the words, *al-ḥamdu lillāhi rabbi al-'ālamīn* and *rabbanā wa laka al-ḥamd* are your chance to bring God's blessings and grace to mind, then *subḥāna rabbiya al-'aẓīm* and *subḥāna rabbiya al-a'lā* are your opportunity to think and reflect on God's greatness and creative power.

Put your prayer to use for the good of both your life on Earth and your life in the Hereafter. Be one of those people who, when they prostrate themselves and utter words of praise, their entire bodies, their minds, and their hearts are filled with thanksgiving.

21

Red Key No. 3: 'Blessed Greeting to God'

AL-TAḤIYĀTU LILLĀH WA AL-ṢALAWĀTU WA AL-ṬAYYIBĀTU

Do you realise what it means to be greeting God Himself? Can you see what a precious privilege it is to be able to sit in His very presence, there at the cosmic lote tree (*sidrat al-muntahā*) as He looks upon you from His Throne of Almightiness and you say 'Blessed greetings to God'?

The stages of the prayer preceding this have simply been preparing you for this momentous step. Their only purpose has been to give you the spiritual charge you need to traverse the inner expanses that will bring you to where you are now, and to receive the extraordinary reward you now enjoy: that of greeting God Himself. Given the wonderful situation in which you now find yourself, live the moment to the fullest. Be fully aware that it is God Himself that you are addressing when you say, 'I salute you, O God!' You are 'live on air' with the Creator of the Universe, Exalted and Majestic, without any intermediary or go-between!

Even if this encounter were not going to be followed by still another reward (which it is, in fact), the encounter in and of itself, if you truly experience the joy it offers, is a pleasure beyond all pleasures, a prize matched by no other. The words of greeting I speak of are as follows:

> *Al-taḥiyātu lillāh wa al-ṣalawātu wa al-ṭayyibātu.*
> Blessed greetings to God! Fragrant prayers to God Most High!
> *Al-salāmu ʿalayka ayyuhā al-nabiyyu wa raḥmatu Allāhi wa barakātuh.*
> Peace be upon you, O Prophet, and God's mercy and blessings!
> *Al-salāmu ʿalaynā*
> Peace be upon us,
> *wa ʿalā ʿibādillāh al-ṣāliḥīn.*
> and upon all God's righteous servants!

The greetings summarised above actually constitute a set of four separate greetings, each of them distinct from the others. In the first we salute our Almighty Creator alone ('Blessed greetings to God! Fragrant prayers to God Most High!'). In the second we encounter His gracious Messenger ('Peace be upon you, O Prophet, and God's mercy and blessings!'). It is only after this encounter that we begin to receive the 'grand prize' through a greeting addressed to ourselves ('Peace be upon us'). The sacred procession of greetings is then concluded by a prayer for peace 'upon all God's righteous servants'.

These four greetings are interspersed by a number of 'open spaces' which, as we have seen, constitute a critical linguistic element of the Salah. Given the expansive wording of these four greetings, the time it takes us to utter each of them allows us to absorb the import of the preceding phrases and to conjure their subtle nuances.

Let us imagine now that these prayers and greetings came in brief, rapid-fire succession: 'Greetings to God, peace be upon the Prophet, and upon us, and upon the righteous.' Or, even more to the point, they might read, 'Greetings to God, to His Messenger, to us and to the righteous.' Notice that the two 'quick' versions suggested here leave out nothing of the intended meaning. However, they deprive us of numerous subtle dimensions found in the original text.

The abbreviated form of expression that I have proposed here gives us no opportunity to take in the wondrousness of the extraordinary position in which we find ourselves, to ponder its significance, and to soak up the showers of blessings and mercy bathing us from head to toe. It also prevents us from appreciating the immediacy of the Divine response we are receiving.

In order to experience the blessings of this greeting more fully, try removing the vowel sound from the ends of certain words so as to make them last longer. You might say, for example: *al-taḥiyyātu. . . lillāh . . . wa al-ṣalawāt . . . al-ṭayyibāt . . .*

The same approach could be applied to the greeting we deliver to the Messenger in the words, *al-salāmu 'alayka ayyuhā al-nabī*, 'Peace be upon you, O Prophet.' When we invoke God's peace upon the person most beloved to God and to the entire Muslim community, we open ourselves to two sources of happiness that should never be taken for granted. We should proceed slowly, and not move on until we have fully experienced the exhilarating impact of each phrase we have uttered. The first source of happiness is the act of greeting the Messenger of God as though he were directly before us, while the second is the response we receive from the Prophet, who has been brought back to life to return our greeting. As the Prophet is reported to have said, 'Whenever anyone greets me, God will restore me to life in order for me to return his or her greeting of peace.'[36]

Even more amazing and joyous is the knowledge that God Almighty joins His Prophet in this gracious response. For He Himself, when you pray for or greet His Prophet, greets and blesses you in return. This is affirmed in more than one Divine saying uttered on the lips of the Prophet, who said, 'Pray for me especially on Fridays. The angel Gabriel once came to me and, speaking on God's behalf, told me, "Whenever any Muslim on Earth prays for you once [on Friday], My angels and I will pray for that Muslim ten times over".'[37]

What a greeting of peace! What a prayer! What a reward! Can you even begin to imagine what it means for God to pray for you, and for millions upon millions of God's angels to join Him in this prayer at His command? Do you perceive what a wonder it is for these sacred prayers for blessing upon you to be repeated ten times over whenever you pray for the Prophet, whether during prayer or at any other time?

22

Red Key No. 4: 'Peace be upon us...'

AL-SALĀMU ʿALAYNĀ WA ʿALĀ ʿIBĀDILLĀHI AL-ṢĀLIḤĪN

These words are more than just a greeting. They are a symbol of the grand prize you have received as a result of entering God's presence and greeting Him and His gracious Messenger. If you paid a visit to a president or a monarch, and you find that, upon leaving his palace or mansion, he had left you a gift at the door, you would be astonished. Being from a head of state, moreover, it would be no ordinary gift, but one that reflects the giver's status and social position.

What gift might one expect, then, from the Maker of kings and presidents, the Maker of the heavens and the earth, if you came to pay Him your respects? The Messenger of God declared that we would receive a reward, or rewards, for every greeting of peace we deliver to anyone on Earth. Hence, the gift you would receive from God Almighty would inevitably exceed anything you could ask or think, whether in heaven or on earth, from the time Adam was created until the day when human beings are raised from the dead.

> If anyone says, *al-salāmu 'alaykum*, 'Peace be upon you,' ten good deeds will be credited to him. If one says, *al-salāmu 'alaykum wa raḥmatu Allāh*, 'Peace be upon you, and the mercy of God,' twenty good deeds will be recorded in his favor. And if someone says, *al-salāmu 'alaykum wa raḥmatu Allāhi wa barakātuh*, 'Upon you be peace and the blessings and mercy of God,' thirty good deeds will be recorded in his favor.[38]

When you utter this double greeting in your prayer, you are bound to experience a double honour: the honour of receiving the unbounded Divine peace as it is poured out upon you, your family, and your loved ones (*al-salāmu 'alaynā*), bathing you and them in God's mercy, kindness and tranquility; and the honour of being showered with Divine favour for having called down peace upon 'all God's righteous servants.'

Again, never lose sight of the fact that the peace you invoke in this supplication is not for you alone; rather, you are invoking peace upon 'us'. There is a world of difference between invoking peace on yourself alone, and invoking it on yourself together with everyone around you: on loved ones near and far, relatives and strangers, believers the world over, and countless groups of people who are included among 'God's righteous servants'.

Lastly, remember that in all these supplications you are not giving only; rather, you are receiving as well. With every word you say, you should make certain that you receive your reward for it without delay.

> After saying, *al-taḥiyātu lillāh* ('greetings to God'), wait and enjoy receiving the response. After saying *al-ṣalawāt al-ṭayyibātu* ('Fragrant prayers to God'), wait and enjoy receiving the response. After praying, *Allahumma ṣalli 'alā Muḥammad* ('O God, pray for Muḥammad'), wait and enjoy receiving the response. And after saying, *wa 'alā Āli Muḥammad* ('and upon his family'), wait and enjoy receiving the response.

And now, after all you have come to know and understand, do you still feel, as you rise for prayer, as though you are just fulfilling a duty that you would rather be free of? Or do you feel as though you are coming to receive a prize greater than any the world could offer, and to exercise a right more wonderful than any other one could enjoy? If you do not emerge from prayer feeling as though you have been born again, then you have missed its true meaning.

23

A Session for Supplication and Private Worship

Supplication or petition (Arabic, *du'ā'*) is a simplified form of Salah. It is marked by the spirit of Salah, but lacks the formal framework, protocols, preparations, procedures and specified times. It is a type of light, free-flowing prayer that can be offered anywhere, at any time, and under any circumstances.

English speakers, I might note, use the word 'prayer' to refer to both what the Arabs call Salah, or canonical prayer, and what is termed *du'a'*, or supplication. This merging of terms suggests that as long as the person concerned is addressing God, then his or her speech constitutes a form of prayer. Perhaps this helps to explain why the language the Prophet employed when engaged in supplication, which was always addressed to God, was clearly distinguishable from his regular style of conversation, which was addressed to others around him. Critics familiar with Islamic texts and well-versed in Arabic literary styles and rhetoric will notice that despite the beauty and eloquence of the Prophet's day-to-day speech, the language he used in prayers of supplication is nevertheless more moving and filled with pathos, more rhythmic, more rhetorically masterful, and more captivating than the language he used in everyday conversation. Similarly, the discerning critic can distinguish between the language used in extra-Qur'anic Divine utterances transmitted by the Prophet (*al-aḥādīth al-qudsiyyah*), and the language the Prophet used in day-to-day conversation.

Like the Hadith Qudsi (Divine sayings uttered by the Prophet), the language, tone and cadence of his supplications have a spiritual aura about them as though Heaven had taken part in their formulation. When teaching his Companions such prayers, the Messenger of God made certain that they memorised them word for word, and he would alert them to the importance of preserving their original wording exactly as he had conveyed it to them. So adamant was he on this point that he once corrected one of his Companions simply for replacing the word 'Prophet' with the word 'Messenger', even though both terms refer clearly to the same person.

> Al-Barā' Ibn 'Āzib related the following incident: 'The Prophet (pbuh) once said, "Before going to bed, perform your ablution as though you were going to pray. Then lie down on your right side and say, 'O God, I have surrendered myself unto You, and directed my face toward You. I have entrusted my concerns to You and placed myself under Your protection. I do all this in a desire for You and in awe of Your power. There is no refuge or protection from You but in You. I have believed in Your book which You have revealed, and in Your Prophet whom You have sent.' Then if you should die before you wake, you will die in the pristine, natural state in which you came into this world. So let these be

> the last words you utter." So, I repeated the words back to him (pbuh), and when I got to the part that says, "I have believed in Your book which You have revealed," I said, "Your Messenger" instead of "Your Prophet." And he said to me, "No, 'and Your Prophet whom You have sent'".'[39]

Hence, the Prophet taught his Companions certain prayers of supplication in the same way he taught them passages from the Qur'an, insisting that they be learned verbatim, with no additions or deletions. This is illustrated in the following incident:

> According to Ibn 'Abbās, the Messenger of God used to teach them a certain prayer of supplication in the same way he would teach them a *sūrah* from the Qur'an. He said, 'Say: O God, we seek Your protection (with one version of the account reading, "I seek Your protection") from the torment of Hell. I seek Your protection from the torment of the grave. I seek Your protection from the wiles of the Antichrist, and I seek Your protection from the temptations and allures of both life and death.' [40]

And:

> The Messenger of God (pbuh) taught us *al-tashahhud* (*al-taḥiyātu lillāh*), which includes greetings to be uttered to God and others, in the same way he taught us *sūrahs* of the Qur'an. [41]

24

Computing Profits and Losses

Have you ever, after one of the five daily prayers, taken pencil and paper and recorded the number of moments when you felt you were actually speaking to God, when it seemed that real communication was taking place, when your heart quaked or a tremor went through you, if even just once, or for a single second or fraction of a second? In other words, have you ever tried to estimate, if only in the most approximate way, how much you have benefited from your time in prayer?

> 'Ammār ibn Yāsir once related that the Messenger of God (pbuh) had said, 'Some people come away from Salah with only one-tenth, one-ninth, one-eighth, one seventh, one-sixth, one-fifth, one fourth, one-third, or one-half having been counted in their favor.'[42]

Try not to conclude a single prayer without having experienced a sense of real communion with God, however briefly. If you fail in the first *rak'ah*, try again in the second, then the third, then the fourth. If you fail during the obligatory ones try in the Sunnah-based *rak'ahs*. If you fail at the dawn prayer, then try again during the noon prayer, the mid-afternoon prayer, the sundown prayer, and the last evening prayer. Do not let a day go by without your having wept during at least one of your prayers, without having trembled if even for a second or a fraction of a second, or having experienced the joy of making contact with God Almighty. This is the least a believer might hope to experience. And if you manage to experience more than this, rejoice in what you have added to your store of heavenly treasure.

Department stores often announce raffles for valuable prizes as a way of encouraging people to buy their merchandise. All customers have to do is fill out a ticket before leaving the store with their address and telephone number so that, in the event that they win the prize, they can be contacted. When you enter into Salah, you are stepping into a Divine storehouse in which you have the chance to fill out untold numbers of 'tickets', each of which qualifies you for a different prize. One of the many differences between the prizes given out by commercial establishments and the ones awarded by the Divine storehouse is that when it comes to the latter, you do not simply stand a chance of winning; you are guaranteed to win not only one prize, but all the prizes available – if, that is, you succeed in filling out its tickets in the right way.

When you pray, you embark on an investment enterprise that guarantees you more profit than any other on the face of the earth, and at the least cost to you. This mammoth venture requires next to no capital. When you distribute *zakāh*, you pay at least 2.5 per cent of your liquid assets. In order to go on the pilgrimage, you have to set aside a considerable budget, including the cost of travel, lodging and other expenses. And when you fast the month of Ramadan, you're obliged to abstain from food, drink and numerous other licit pleasures during the daytime hours, and donate fast-breaking charity (*ṣadaqat al-fiṭr*) at the end of the month on behalf of each person in your household. As for prayer, all it costs is the water you consume in completing your ritual ablution and the time it takes you to pray. That's it: no fees, no taxes! And in return, you make huge profits that are deposited immediately in your spiritual account. In fact, you collect some of them directly even before finishing your prayer. These immediate profits include: peace of mind, improved health, tranquility, clarity of thought, and a sense of renewal. Some of them, by contrast, are wrapped up and sent in elegant-looking packages either to your address in this world (success, blessing, well-being, answered prayers) or to your address in the life to come (having sins erased, and having countless good deeds added to your record).

Is not an enterprise like this important enough to merit preparation of a profit-loss ledger? The losses of which I speak here are not, of course, the kind we normally think of. They involve no reduction in capital. Rather, they simply involve a diminution in the profits you might have been able to add to your existing capital. As for the 'capital' you already possess, it will remain untouched unless, God forbid, your prayers are performed in a spirit of hypocrisy, showing off and deceit.

Given this investment-based understanding of spiritual disciplines, perhaps you can begin doing an estimate of the profits you have made at the end of every prayer, as well as the profits you forfeited by allowing preoccupations to distract you from your worship.

THE JEWELS YOU HAVE GLEANED THROUGH PRAYER

Do not forget as you review your prayer ledger to go back to the five 'lines' summarised in an earlier discussion: The line of time, the line of the tongue, the line of the body, the line of the heart, and the line of action. Remember also to conduct your review based on the number of minutes you spent in prayer. If you finished two *rak'ahs* in only two or three minutes, then you did not really pray, and you should go back and give it another try, since you barely had time to recite the words of the prayer, and did not give yourself the chance to grasp their meanings, hence, to translate this grasp into concrete responses.

Every Muslim should set up a simple scale against which to measure the approximate number of 'points' he or she scored in any given prayer. After all, the individual worshipper is the only person capable of knowing how his/her prayer was. You should remember, of course, that the actual fruit borne by a given prayer can never be known precisely by anyone but the One who knows all things, and to whom we addressed ourselves in the prayer in question.

After each Salah ask yourself the following questions:

1) When I raised my hands and uttered the opening *Allahu Akbar*, did I feel as though I was leaving everything behind and being ushered into another world exalted above the earthly realm?
2) How many times did my utterance of the words, *Allahu Akbar*, 'God is greater...' wrest me out of a state of distraction and bring me back to the world of prayer, lifting me to heights of ecstasy far removed from the trivialities and distractions of the world below, and into the presence of the One who is 'greater'?

3) How many times did the Divine name *al-Raḥmān* bathe me in light from above, enabling me to sense fresh mercy and grace descending upon me? And how continuously did the Divine name *al-Raḥīm* bathe me in light, awakening me to the mercy and compassion that extend from time immemorial to time immemorial, and purifying me body and soul?
4) How many Qur'anic expressions did I recite from the *Fātiḥah* (such as *al-ḥamdu lillāhi, rabbi al-'ālamīn, Māliki yawmi al-dīn, iyyāka na'budu*) in such a way that I saw God's greatness manifesting itself before me and changing something inside me as I recited?
5) How many times, after reciting verses from the *Fātiḥah* or some other *sūrah*, did I leave myself enough time to take them in, reflect on them, and digest their significance?
6) Did I bring to mind my immediate family, relatives and friends, both Muslim and non-Muslim, as well as my enemies, Muslim and non-Muslim, as I prayed, 'Guide us the straight way....', embracing them all in this gracious supplication? And did I experience the sweetness of my reward for calling down Divine guidance and wisdom on them?
7) How many times during my bows and prostrations did I try to fill the 'virtual space' after each *Allāhu Akbar* and *tasbīḥā*? How many seconds did I give myself to fill this space?
8) How many of the following 'red buttons' did I press during my prayer? And how many times did I sense a spiritual current reaching deep inside me, shaking me to the core, causing my heart to tremble or moving me to tears?

- The 'unto You alone do we turn for aid' (*iyyāka nasta'īn*) button: How many seconds did I give myself after this phrase to remind myself of the nature of the request I am making and the type of aid I seek; to conjure images of myself and all the other people included in the plural pronoun 'we'?
- The 'blessed greetings to God' (*al-taḥiyātu lillāh*) button: How long did it take me to utter this phrase with the proper prolongation of the vowel sounds and a pause afterwards, as well as the phrases that follow it: *al-ṣalawāt wa al-ṭayyibāt*, 'fragrant prayers to God'? Did I give myself sufficient time to take in the joy and wonder of entering God's presence, greeting Him with the words He Himself had taught me, and being greeted by Him in return?
- The 'Peace be upon you, O Prophet, and God's mercy and blessings!' (*al-salamu 'alayka ayyuhā al-nabiyyu wa raḥmatu Allāhi wa barakātuh*) button: How long did it take me to utter this greeting, particularly the prolonged vowels in the words *al-salāmu* ('peace'), *Allāhi* ('God') and *barakātuh* ('blessings')? Given the time lapses afforded by these prolongations, as well as the open temporal space following the greeting, did I experience the double exhilaration of calling down blessings and peace upon the Prophet and receiving his response?
- The 'peace be upon us, and upon all God's righteous servants' (*al-salāmu 'alaynā wa 'alā 'ibādillāhi al-ṣāliḥīn*) button: As I called down peace upon myself, those I care for, and generation after generation of God's righteous servants wherever they happen to be or have been, in whatever age they have lived,

did I feel a gentle shower of sacred, pristine peace descending upon me and upon them, cleansing me and them of everything that might harm us? Did I feel myself being showered with more grace as I received Heaven's generous reward for every greeting I had offered? Did I feel myself being relieved of any kind of headache, illness, weariness, burden or anxiety?

9) Was I able, in the voluntary, Sunnah-based prayers, to make up for what I may have failed to achieve in the mandatory prayer cycles? Or vice-versa?
10) And lastly, did I succeed in this new exercise in patience and perseverance? Did I feel new spiritual energy surging through me? Did I sense that some change, however slight, had taken place in me on the level of physical and mental well-being, moral strength, perseverance and wisdom?

THE PRAYER GEMS YOU MISSED

After praying, ask yourself the following questions:

1) How many utterances of Allahu Akbar, 'God is greater,' went by without helping me in concentrating on what I was saying?
2) How many verses of the Qur'an did I recite without being mindful of their meanings?
3) How many expressions of praise (*subḥāna rabbiya al-'aẓīm, subḥāna rabbiya al-a'lā*) during bows and prostrations did I simply repeat parrot-fashion without enjoying their sweetness or the richness of their meaning, and without making good use of the open space following them?

4) How many times did I allow myself to straighten or fiddle with my clothing or hair while coming down into a prostration? How many times did I move my hands or any other part of my body unnecessarily?
5) How many times was I distracted from my prayer by designs, shapes or colours on the prayer mat or elsewhere in my immediate surroundings?
6) How many times had I absented myself from my prayer by this or that worldly or mundane concern?
7) How many times was my attention drawn away from worship by a side conversation nearby, the sound of a television or radio, a ringing telephone, a doorbell or a knock at the door?
8) Which of the five 'lines' of prayer did I fail to handle properly in my prayer: time, the tongue, the body, the heart, and, later, action?
9) Do I feel that the prayer gave me added strength to resist engaging in actions that would be inconsistent with the words I spoke to God in prayer?
10) Do I feel that I passed the 'course' prayer offers in determination, perseverance and patience? Or did I come out of prayer no different than I was before entering it?

***

Lastly, when you lay your head on the pillow at night and recite the traditional prayers of supplication passed down on the Prophet's authority, try to do a quick review of all the 'prayer points' you recorded for yourself over the course of the day, especially the ones associated with the 'red buttons.' Then compare these with the total you achieved the previous day in order to see whether you have made any progress in your daily score. If you have regressed, work on correcting yourself the next day in such a way that the overall trend will be upward rather than downward. At the end of each week, give yourself a final rating for the entire week and compare this rating with the one you got the week before. In this way you can make sure that your investments bring steadily growing dividends.

25

Let Your Whole Life be a Prayer

According to the Prophet's account of *laylat al-mi'rāj*, the night when he was taken up to the heavenly realm and received instructions from on high to legislate prayer for the Muslim community, the initial command he was given was for us to pray fifty times a day. The Prophet kept pleading with his Lord to reduce the number of required daily prayers until they numbered only five. And I used to wonder, as you may have as well: How on earth would we have been able to perform fifty prayers a day? Would we have had time to do anything else? When would we have been able to eat, drink, and sleep, read and write, talk to each other, work, go on visits, and so much else?

Later, however, when I came to understand the nature of prayer and the impact it has on the person who prays, I could see that prayer is life, and that life, in all its details and minutiae, is made up of various kinds of prayer:

- When you wake up and discover with gratitude that you are still alive after the temporary 'death' of sleep, you are at prayer.
- When you look into children's faces and marvel at the way they grow and develop both physically and mentally, with new skills, new words and new modes of expression emerging with every passing day, you are at prayer.
- When you teach your children to do good and invite them to faith in God 'with wisdom and goodly exhortation' (*al-Naḥl* 16:125), whether or not they follow your advice, you are at prayer.
- When you forgive your brother, your sister, your colleague or your neighbour from the heart for some wrong he or she has done you and if, further, you apologise to him or her as though you were the offending party, you are at prayer.
- When someone curses or insults you but you don't respond in kind, counting it instead as a trial to be borne in the hope of receiving a reward from God, you are at prayer.
- When you leave a gathering where people are engaged in backbiting because you find yourself unable to change the course of the conversation or defend the person being slandered, you are at prayer.
- When you ask God to guide a non-Muslim to the straight path you are at prayer.
- When you show a non-Muslim the mercy, compassion, gentleness and love of Islam, treating him or her in a civilised, polite and cordial manner, you are at prayer.
- When you keep the laws of the land you live in, even if it is not a Muslim country, demonstrating a grateful

attitude and fulfilling your financial, social and moral obligations toward it, you are at prayer.

- When you are surrounded by corruption on all sides and denounce it in your heart even though you see no way to change it through your words or actions, you are at prayer.
- When you do your utmost to please your family and others around you, whether or not your efforts are successful, you are at prayer.
- When you believe heartily that God has only your best interests at heart and, hence, you think only well of God no matter what doubts your inner demons assail you with, you are at prayer.
- When you praise God for both blessings and afflictions, you are at prayer.
- When you avert your gaze from the worldly temptations that surround you, you are at prayer.
- When you steadfastly endure illness, poverty, tragedy, or other difficult life circumstances, you are at prayer.
- When you spare a life or help to spare a life you are at prayer.
- When you share in the concerns, sufferings and sorrows of Muslims and non-Muslims in a country other than your own, if even simply by raising your voice in protest or by making supplication for them, you are at prayer.
- When you visit someone who is ill, you are at prayer. After all, did not your Prophet instruct you to perform a ritual ablution before visiting an ill person?
- When you go to bed and rest your body from the stress of a long day in preparation for a new day of fruitful, constructive activity, you are at prayer. After all, did not your Prophet instruct you to perform a ritual ablution

before sleeping, as if sleep were itself a kind of prayer?
- And lastly, when you do a personal accounting of your day before bed, noting the things you did right and the ways you failed, you are also at prayer.

In short, when you look at the world through the lens of a worshipper, you see that your entire life is a prayer. So, do not miss any of life's opportunities to worship, opportunities that present themselves at every turn. Life's infinite particulars are 'words' that bespeak the grandeur of the Creator: extolling His power, praising His bounty and grace, announcing His blessings, and reminding His servants to direct themselves continuously to Him and never to lose sight of the fact that they are ever and always engaged in some form of worship.

If someone offends you, do not be angry or bitter. Instead, let it be an opportunity for praise and worship. Say to yourself, 'Both this other person and I are God's creatures. What a superb paintbrush it was that could grant such a distinct personality, appearance and temperament to each of the billions of souls on Earth!'

Let everything you encounter, everything you hear, everything you see around you be an occasion for praise to God. Who am I to pronounce something or someone ugly when everything and everyone is one of God's creations? Even the lightning that blinds my sight, the thunder that makes me tremble with fear, and the terror and dread that Nature's cataclysms can inspire, give rise within me to exclamations of praise that bring me all the closer to God.

Whether you are still or in motion, seated or standing, eating or drinking, making money or spending it, listening or speaking – in short, whatever situation you find yourself in – be part of this vast Universe, which is unceasingly, tirelessly engaged in remembrance, praise, thanksgiving, and worship. For as long as you are alive, you are at prayer. So, let these golden rules be your guides in life:

- Do not take a step outside your home to 'fix' the world around you without first taking a step inside yourself to 'fix' your relationship with the world to come.
- Do not waste an hour of your time without imagining that you have less than this hour left to live on Earth.
- Do not cleanse your bodily members through ritual ablution without also working to cleanse yourself from within.
- Do not utter a word in prayer without making up your mind to let your actions bear witness to its truth.
- Do not bow your head reverently in prayer without bowing your will humbly in daily life.
- Do not leave the mosque the same person you were when you went in.
- Do not bid farewell to the month of Ramadan without having bidden farewell to some form of disobedience and welcomed in some new form of obedience.
- Do not perform a good deed with your right hand without having warded off some evil with your left.
- Do not slaughter a sacrificial animal in the hope of drawing nearer to Heaven without 'slaughtering' an act of disobedience that might draw you nearer to Hell.
- Do not spend a penny needlessly without remembering those who have died in search of the wherewithal to escape cold, illness or hunger.
- Do not fill your glass to the brim if you know you will only drink half its contents.
- Do not waste a drop of water without remembering

those who die daily of thirst.

- Do not place a bite of food in your mouth without remembering those who have died for lack of it.
- Do not dispose of the leftovers from a meal while forgetting that God could deprive you of everything on your table.
- Do not enjoy the fruits of this world without longing to enjoy the fruits of the world to come.
- Do not take as much pleasure in what you have acquired, then spent, as in what you have given, and thus kept.
- Rather than being irritated that you do not have the right shoes to wear, grieve for those who have no feet on which to wear them.
- Do not grumble when an appliance or piece of furniture in your home breaks, remembering that there are people who have no homes at all.
- Do not sprinkle salt on your food without sprinkling sugar on your words.
- Say nothing negative about anyone without bearing in mind that someone might say the same about you.
- Address neither of your parents with disrespect, knowing you will hear similar words of disrespect some day from your own children.
- Despise no one of lower standing, knowing that God has far more reason to despise you than you have to despise the person before you.
- Do not ask God to pardon you for offending against Him without first pardoning those who have offended against you.
- Do not allow so much as a speck of hatred to steal into your heart without inviting a vast share of love to come in as well.

- Before praying for those you love, pray for those you are not certain you love, or whose love for you is not certain.
- Do not be daunted by trials that call for patient perseverance, but rest assured of the reward that awaits you and the relief that is certain to come in due time.

And lastly, do not forget to act on the injunction of the gracious Prophet to 'worship God as though you saw Him, and count yourself among the dead. Remember God at every stone and every tree, and should you commit an evil deed, perform a good one alongside it: for a secret transgression, a secret good deed, and for a public transgression, a public good deed'.[43]

KL

With every breath you take, remember that your entire life is a prayer. In all circumstances, and wherever you go, be as pure in spirit as you are in body after preparing for the Salah. And be as consciously grateful to your Lord as is every cell in your body, every joint, muscle and pore without conscious awareness.

Know that the way you manage prayer reflects, and will be reflected in, the way you manage your life. Islam's first pillar, the testimony of faith (*shahādah*), is a means of ensuring your well-being in the life to come, while prayer, its second pillar, is a means of ensuring your welfare in both the life to come and your life on Earth. This book is intended to furnish you with a set of keys with which to open up the storehouses of your mind and heart, to go soaring through the worlds of your imagination with God, and to set sail on the seas of discovery.

O God, *I ask Your forgiveness for any sin of which I have repented only to lapse into it once again. I ask Your forgiveness for the times I have given You something of myself, only unwittingly to take it back. I ask Your forgiveness for using the strength with which You have blessed me to commit acts of disobedience. I ask Your forgiveness for allowing the good things through which I have sought You to draw me away toward what is other than You.*

Endnotes

1: An Appointment with God

1. Narrated by Muslim.

3: From Duty to Privilege

2. Narrated by Aḥmad on the authority of ʿAmr Ibn Shuʿayb on the authority of his father, to whom it was narrated by his father.
3. Narrated by Muslim on the authority of Jābir Ibn ʿAbd Allāh.
4. Narrated on the authority of Ibn ʿUmar, and declared authentic by Muḥammad Nāṣir al-Dīn al-Albānī in his book Silsilat al-Aḥādīth al-Ṣaḥiḥah.
5. Narrated on the authority of ʿUqbah Ibn ʿĀmir, and declared authentic by al-Albānī in Ṣaḥīḥ al-Targhīb wa al-Tarhīb.
6. Narrated by al-ʿIrāqī on the authority of Bilāl Ibn Rabāḥ.

4: The Satisfaction of Waking Up Early for Prayer

7. Narrated by al-Bukhārī on the authority of Abū Hurayrah.

6: Why Do We Pray?

8. Narrated on the authority of 'Abd Allāh Ibn 'Amr, declared authentic by al-Albānī in his Ṣaḥīḥ al-Jāmi' al-Ṣaghīr wa Ziyādatuh.
9. Narrated on the authority of Mālik Ibn Ḥuwayrith al-Laythī, and declared authentic by al-Albānī in Ṣaḥīḥ al-Jāmi'.
10. Narrated on the authority of 'Abd Allāh Ibn Mas'ūd, and declared authentic by al-Albānī in Ṣaḥīḥ al-Targhīb.
11. Narrated by Ibn Mājah on the authority of Abū Hurayrah.

7: The Rhythm of Prayer and the Rhythm of Life

12. Narrated by al-Bukhārī on the authority of Abū Hurayrah.

9: The Call to Prayer and Its Ten Wonders

13. Narrated by Aḥmad on the authority of Abū al-Dardā'.

10: The Two Ritual Ablutions

14. Narrated by Aḥmad on the authority of Abū Hurayrah, and declared authentic by al-Albānī.
15. Narrated on the authority of Abū Hurayrah in Mishkāt al-Maṣābīḥ and declared authentic by al-Albānī.
16. Narrated by Muslim on the authority of Abū Hurayrah.
17. TafsÏr al-Qur~ubÏ, Part 1, p. 39.

11: Communal Prayer: The Key to Advancement and Civilisation

18. Narrated on the authority of 'Ā'ishah, and declared authentic by al-Albānī in Silsilat al-Aḥādīth al-Ṣaḥiḥah.
19. Narrated on the authority of 'Umar Ibn al-Khaṭṭāb, and declared authentic by al-Albānī in Ẓilāl al-Jannah fī TakhrÏj al-Sunnah.

12: The Friday *Khuṭbah* (Sermon): A Course in Development

20. Narrated by Aḥmad on the authority of Abū Hurayrah.

13: The Five Lines of Prayer

21. Narrated by al-Safārīnī al-Hanbalī on the authority of 'Abd Allāh Ibn 'Abbās in Sharḥ Kitāb al-Shihāb.
22. Narrated by Abū Dāwūd on the authority of 'Ubayd Ibn Khālid al-Sulamī and declared authentic by al-Albānī.

16: The New Language of the Qur'an

23. For more detail on this topic, see the introduction to Part 1 of my book entitled, Al-Mu'jizah (Washington, DC: IIIT, 2012).

17: Open Language and "Fertile Spaces"

24. Narrated by Muslim on the authority of 'Ā'ishah.

18: The Role of the *Fātiḥah*

25. In other words, the parts of the *Fātiḥah* that involve praise to God ('Praise is due to God, the Lord of the Worlds') and affirmation of His mercy ('the Most Gracious, Most Merciful') concern God; while the expressions of worship ('You Alone do we worship') and requests for aid ('You Alone do we seek for aid') and guidance ('Guide us the straight way') involve God's servants.
26. For a more detailed discussion of this point, see the section on the *Fātiḥah* in Part 2 of my book Al-Mu'jizah (Washington, DC: IIIT, 2015), pp. 51-92.
27. Narrated by al-Bukhārī on the authority of 'Ubādah Ibn al-Ṣāmit.
28. This is detailed in my discussion of the *Fātiḥah* in Part 2 of Al-Mu'izah, pp. 51-92.
29. Narrated by al-Bukhārī on the authority of Qatādah.

19: Red Key No. 2: 'You Alone Do We Worship, and unto You Alone Do We Turn for Aid'

30. Narrated by Muslim on the authority of Abū Hurayrah.
31. 'Abd al-Ṣabūr Shāhīn, Tārīkh al-Qur'ān (Cairo: Dār al-Qalam, 1961), p. 175.

20: The Centrality of Bowing and Prostration

32. An alternative reading is: 'Tell me what action most meets with God's favor.'
33. Narrated by both al-Bukhārī and Muslim on the authority of Mi'dān Ibn Abī Ṭalḥah.
34. Narrated on the authority of al-Nu'mān Ibn Murrah, and declared authentic by al-Albānī in Ṣaḥīḥ al-Targhīb.
35. Narrated on the authority of Abū Hurayrah, and declared authentic by al-Albānī in Ṣaḥīḥ al-Targhīb.

21: Red Key No. 3: 'Blessed Greeting to God'

36. Narrated by Ibn Taymiyah in Majmū' al-Fatāwā, and by al-Nawawī on the authority of Abū Hurayrah.
37. Narrated on the authority of Anas Ibn Mālik, and declared 'good' by al-Albāni in Ṣaḥīḥ al-Targhīb.

22: Red Key No. 4: 'Peace be upon us...'

38. Narrated on the authority of Suhayl Ibn Ḥanīf and declared authentic by al-Albānī in Ṣaḥīḥ al-Targhīb.

23: A Session for Supplication and Private Worship

39. Narrated by both al-Bukharī and Muslim.
40. Narrated by Muslim.
41. Narrated by Ibn Mājah on the authority of 'Abd Allāh Ibn 'Abbās, and declared authentic by al-Albānī. A version of this Ḥadith passed down on the authority of 'Abd Allāh Ibn 'Umar adds the words, 'He did not want a single word to be added or removed.

24: Computing Profits and Losses

42. Narrated by Abū Dāwūd and al-Nasā'ī on the authority of 'Ammār Ibn Yāsir and declared authentic by al-Albānī.

25: Let Your Whole Life be a Prayer

43. Narrated on the authority of Mu'ādh Ibn Jabal, and declared 'good' by al-Albānī in Ṣaḥīḥ al-Targhīb.

Index

A
abridgement (*qasr*), 93
Abū al-Dardā', 68
Abū Dawūd, 68
Academy of Contemporary (Muslim) Preachers, 76-77
acceptance of others, 7, 42, 60, 65, 69
adhān, 46-53, 91
adults, 16
Ā'ishah, 66
al-Albānī, Shaykh, 61
al-Rahīm, 23, 102, 104, 107-11, 113
al-Rahmān, 23, 52, 57, 102, 104-105, 107-111, 113
al-Sulamī, Ubayy Abd al-Rahmān, 57
angel Gabriel, 42, 92-94, 130
angels, 11, 51, 58, 62-63, 65, 73, 98
appearance, 55, 62, 77-78, 82, 92, 149
Arabic, 21, 58, 62-63, 70-72, 90, 92, 96, 98, 103, 105, 109, 120, 134
Arabs, 38, 49-50, 90, 92, 96, 103, 134
assimilation (*idghām*), 93
athar al-sujūd, 32
atshān (thirsty), 109
attention, 7, 11, 23, 35, 43, 52-53, 65, 79, 123, 144
āyah, 96, 104, 114, 120

B
bankruptcy, 56-57
basmalah, 104-108
Bismillah al-Rahmān, al-Rahīm, 23, 104-105, 111
bodily movements, 41, 43, 73

bowing, 31, 57, 98, 122–125, 150
British Accreditation Council, 76, 78–79

C
charity, 13, 56, 139
children, 3–4, 10, 16, 38–39, 42, 77, 118–119, 151
Christianity, 27, 55
civilization, 21, 24, 39–42, 47, 55, 58, 60–66, 69, 76, 79–80
cleanliness, 60–62, 77–78
communal prayer, 46–47, 60–61, 68–69, 76, 78–80, 90
  basic cultural conditions, 78–79
communication with God, 15–16, 84, 106
compassion, 31, 52, 69, 108–110, 141
connection (*wasl*), 93
creativity, 16, 40
Creator, 18, 21, 127–128, 149

D
dawn prayer (*Salāt al-fajr*), 15–18, 33, 37, 67, 138
Day of Judgement, 56
Day of Resurrection, 53, 56, 102, 116
dedication, 21, 69
deliberateness, 7, 22
determination, 12, 20–23, 42, 60, 68–69, 119, 144
Divine
  approval, 13
  attributes, 110
  Character, 23
  gift, 18
  guidance, 117, 141
  inspiration, 48
  invitation, 87
  mercy and compassion, 109, 115
  names, 108, 141
  peace, 132
  perfection, 98
  praise of consecration (takbirat al-ihram), 89
  program, 26
  remembrance (adhkar), 52
  response, 129
  revelation, 47, 92
  reward, 88
  saying, 107, 130, 135
  storehouse, 138
  Sustainer, 93
  utterances, 135
  wisdom, 38, 46, 118, 141
Divinely inspired form, 28, 30
Divinely ordained punishments, 123
duties *vs.* rights, 12–14

E
earth, 9, 11, 18, 24, 28, 48, 65–66, 69, 88, 105–109, 118, 126, 130–131, 149–150, 152
enjoyment, 7–9, 13, 20
enthusiasm, 68–69
equality, 21, 60, 79
evening prayer (*Salāt al-Iishā'*), 30, 33, 36–37, 67, 138

F
Fa'īl, 109–110
fa'lān, 109
familiarity, 4, 26, 41, 46, 57, 70, 90–91, 98, 104
farhān (joyful), 109
fasting, 13, 22, 28, 32
Fātihah (Qur'an's opening *sūrah*)
  Arabic linguistic phenomena, 103
  fundamental meaning, 106, 114
  God Almighty on, 113
  greetings and supplications, 100
  important part of Salah, 50, 52, 99, 102, 104
  open-ended expressions, 101, 117–118
  vowel elongation (Madd) in, 120
five daily prayers, 2, 15, 24, 30, 37, 40–41, 60–61, 64, 68, 71, 137
  benefits, 137–139
five lines of prayer
  essential elements; time, body, tongue, heart, action, 84–86
  preparation, 87
forbidden (*harām*), 13
forms of worship. *See also* Salah, fasting and Hajj (pilgrimage) to Makkah, 3–5, 22
four cycles of prayer (raka'*āt*), 36, 39, 51
freedom, 21, 123
Friday KHUTBAH (sermon)
  day-to-day reality, 71–72
  fundamental role in Islamic society, 73–75
  Imam's role, 74–76
  in Arabic, 71
  in English, 70
  modern-day issues, 69–71
fu'lān, 99

G
generosity, 21, 110
generous person (*karīm*), 110
genitive case (*majrūr*), 105
ghadbān (angry), 109
God Almighty, 3, 6–7, 9, 11, 13, 16, 24, 26–27, 29, 48, 56, 62, 83–84, 92–94, 99–100, 102, 107–108, 110, 113, 115, 122, 125, 128, 130–131, 138. *See also* Creator; Maker, *specific entries*
God is great (*Allāhu kabīr*), 91
'God is greater!' (*Allāhu Akbar*!), 11, 22, 28, 45, 49, 51, 89–91, 98–100, 125, 140–141, 143
God is the greatest (*Allāhu huwa al-akbar*), 91
God's righteous servants' (*'ibādillh al-ṣāliḥīn*), 23, 128
goodly blessings (*al-ṣalawāt al-ṭayyibātu*), 23, 133
Gospel (New Testament), 27
Gospel of Luke, 27
Gospel of Matthew, 27
greetings to God (*al-taḥiyāt lillāh*), 23, 127–129, 133

H
habit, 4, 17, 26, 41, 46, 98, 104, 125
Hadith, 6, 21, 28, 38, 54, 65, 71, 73–74, 86, 88, 98, 135, 154–155, 157
Hadith Qudsi (Divine sayings uttered by Prophet), 135
Hajj or pilgrimage to Makkah, 12, 22, 32, 68, 89, 122
hard thing (*kabīrah*), 6
hatredness, 55, 63, 119
Heaven, 24, 28–29, 42, 65–66, 69, 88, 109, 123, 135, 143, 150
Hebrew Scriptures (Old Testament), 27
highly stressed (*mu'akkadah*) prayers, 37–38
honesty, 21, 60
human weakness, 31–32
humble in spirit (*al-khāsh'iūn*), 6
humble reverence, 6–7, 22–23, 41, 85, 96, 100
humility, 21, 31–32, 60, 62–63, 65, 68

I
Ibn 'Āzib, Al-Barā', 135
ibn al-Khaṭṭāb, 'Umar, 47
Ibn Ka'b, Ubayy, 57
Ibn Majāh, 116
Ibn Mālik, Anas, 116
Ibn Mas'ud, 'Uthman, 57
Ibn Mas'u d, Abd Allah, 6
ill-mannered individual (*wadī'*), 110
imagination, 3, 7, 49, 90, 94, 98–99, 117, 152
imam, 63, 70–71, 73–75, 77, 80
impurities, 31, 56, 58
integrity, 21, 60, 112
International Islamic Accreditation Council, 76
invisible beings (jinn), 48
iqāmah (announcement of communal prayer), 46–47, 52–53, 90
Islam
call to prayer, 49
communal prayer, 80
five pillars, 46
forms of worship, 22
fundamental moral teachings, 74–76
on gift of prayer, 28–29, 119
highly stressed practice, 37
humble reverence, 23–24
masjid, 62
misconception, 6
non-Muslims and, 71, 147
Qur'an's interpretation, 67
rapidity history, 38–40
ritual ablutions, 55
teaching Salah to children, 42
Islamic schooling, 39–40
Islamic tradition, 10, 39

J
jāmi', 63
Jesus, 27
Judaism, 27, 55
Jumu'ah prayer, 70, 73
justice, 6, 21, 32, 60, 85, 119

K
Ka'bah, 122

L
laylat al-mi'rāj (night journey), 49, 146
love, 21, 52, 70, 74, 109, 119, 147, 151–152

M
Maker, 25, 62, 87, 131
masjid, 62
mental concentration, 7, 41
mercy or compassion (*rahmah*), 109
Messenger of God (pbuh), 6, 8, 12, 17, 26, 45, 48, 52, 57, 66–69, 85, 88, 92–93, 95, 103, 110, 113, 120, 123, 125, 129, 131, 135–137
midafternoon prayer (*Salāt al-Asr*), 33, 35
miserly person (*bakhīl*), 110
modesty, 7, 20, 69
Moses, 27
mosque, 16, 46, 60–63, 67–68, 70–71, 73, 75–77, 79–80, 87–88
movements, 7–8, 25–26, 30, 37, 39–41, 43, 67, 73, 106, 124–125
muezzins, 90
Muslim
 ablution performance, 11, 55
 children, 39, 42, 119
 civilization, 24, 40, 80
 communication with god, 107
 fast of Ramadan, 32
 Friday sermon, 71–75
 Hajj, 68
 importance of prayer, 8, 35, 46, 61, 67, 130, 140–141, 146–148
 Islamic faith, 57
 obedience to messenger, 29
 Salah, arguments, 28, 49
 Scripture, 54
 worshippers, 27, 44, 50

N
National Accreditation Council, 80
Natlū, 93
non-Arabs, 70
non-Muslims, 71, 119, 122, 141, 148
noon prayer (*Salat al-Duhr*), 30, 33, 35, 37, 138

O
open-ended expressions, 22, 36, 91, 98–101, 125

P
Paradise, 33, 69, 88, 117, 123
patient endurance, 7, 20, 22
patient perseverance
 in canonical prayer, 20
 Western discourse, 21
pauses (*waqf*), 93
peace of mind, 7, 49, 139

permissible (*ḥalāl*), 13, 72–74
pillars of Islam, 46–53
prayer
  and action, 88
  audible recitation, 35–36
  benefits, 137–139
  cycles, 12, 39, 41–42
  features of, 41–42
  five lines, 81–87, 144
  form of, 28, 134
  golden rules, 150–152
  importance, 8–9
  Islamic call, 45–53
  positions and movements, 43–44
  practice, 20, 23, 67
  prize of, 14
  purpose, 15
  reprogramming of souls, 26–33, 84
  rhythm of life and, 34–36, 48
  stages of, 127
  ten wonders, 45–53
  types, 53, 146–149
Prayer management, 1
pre-Islamic era, 68
precision and mastery, 60
prolongation (madd), 93, 120–121
Prophet Muhammad. *See also* Messenger of God (pbuh)
  biographies of, 38
  on children's prayer, 10
  communication with angel Gabriel, 42
  Companions, 28, 47–48, 136
  empowerment of Islam, 119
  faith community, 47
  on *Fātihah*, 103–104
  on Friday sermons, 63
  God Almighty's communication, 102, 107–108
  golden rules, 152
  on greetings, 129–130
  Islamic call to prayer, 49–51
  on *laylat al-mi'rāj*, 146
  linking earthly instruction to Heaven, 65–66
  on patient perseverance, 20, 23
  on performing Salah, 22, 27, 49, 53, 100, 123–124, 128
  on prayer, 8
  on prayer cycles, 36–38, 71
  on ritual ablution of visiting ill person, 148
  prayers of supplication, 144
  prior to prophethood, 96
  Qur'anic recitation, 74, 95, 110–111, 118
  sayings, 2–3, 23–24, 35, 40, 54–57, 63–64, 68, 88, 98
  Sunnah's importance, 29
  use of language, 134–135
prostration (*athar alsujūd*), 31–32, 43–44, 62–63, 99, 123, 125, 144
punctuality, 60–62, 64

Q

questions, 4, 16, 38–39, 140, 143
Qur'an
  approach to world, 5
  art of rediscovery, 4–5
  chanting, 92–94
  communal recital, 67
  communication of Divine inspiration, 48
  concept of patience in, 21, 23
  Divine utterances, 135
  Fātihah's role, 102–105, 107–108, 116, 118, 120–121, 141
  interpretation and reading, 38, 67
  last *sūrah*, 94
  linguistic style, 50, 95–97
  linking prayer with patient endurance, 7
  performing Salah, 40–41, 43
  prayer of supplication, 136
  questions after prayer, 143
  reading, 92–94
  recitation of, 81–82, 86, 92–94
  reciting, 92–94
  reference to Sunnah, 29
  request for guiding to straight path, 116, 118
  rhetorical style, 74
  on true prayer, 31
  verses, 2–4
  on worship as daily practice, 57

R

Ramadan, 1, 17, 20, 32, 46, 139
rapprochement, 69
red key
  no 1 God is Greater (Allahu Akbar) 89-91 (*See also Fātihah*; Qur'an)
  no 2 'You alone do we worship, and unto You alone do we turn for aid' (*See also* worship), 112–120
  no 3 Blessed Greeting to God', 127–133
reflection, 6–7, 58, 80, 121, 125
repetition, 4, 26, 30, 43, 55, 90, 104, 106
ritual ablutions (*wudū*)
  benefits of, 58–59
  emphasis on cleanliness and orderliness, 58
  of impurities, 55–56
  inward and outward, 55
  Islam's emphasis, 54–55
  meaning of Arabic term, 58
  rite of *tayammum*, or sand ablutions, 58
ritual purity, 54–55, 58, 124, 652

S

Sabr, 21
sahrān (wakeful, watchful), 109
Salah
  analogy of speaking to God, 82–83
  authenticated narratives, 26–27

ayah, 104
bowing and prostrating, 124–125
classification, 6
concept, 10, 25, 107–108
culturally-related aspects, 48–53
dawn prayer, 16, 33
Divine reward for continuous prayer, 88
as Divine storehouse, 138
Fātihah, 102
five simultaneous lines, 84–85
form of worship, 5–6, 22, 28, 41, 67–68
Friday sermon and, 73
ibn Yāsir, ʿAmmār on, 137
intention, 1
linguistic elements, 128
midafternoon prayer, 35
physical movement, 43–44
prayer cycles, 41
prescription, 26
quality or action, 99
questions after prayer, 140–145
rapidity history, 39
reading from paper, 2–3
recitation, 92, 108
ritual ablution, 57–58, 86
school students, 39–41
spirit and body preparation, 144
spiritual prize, 11
Sunnah based prayers, 29, 42
Sunni *versus* Shīʿah Muslims, 67
supplication or petition, 134
takbīrat al-iḥrām, 89, 91
type of phrases, 99–100, 118
with basmalah, 106
Satan, 15, 17, 32, 52–53, 63, 65, 68–69, 90, 122
school of Islam, 39–40
separation (*fasl*), 93
Shīʿah Muslims, 67
solidarity, 20, 62, 65
struggle (jihad), 6, 9
subbūḥ, 98
subḥān, 99
subḥāna, 98
subḥaāna rabbiya al-ʿzīm, 22, 43
subḥāna rabbiyaa al-aʿla, 22, 43
sundown prayer (*Ṣalāt almaghrib*), 30, 33, 35, 37, 67, 138
Sunnah-based cycles, 29, 36–37, 40, 42, 47, 138, 143
Sunni Muslims, 67
Supplication or petition, 134–136
sūrahs, 96–97, 104–105, 108, 136
Sūrat al-Nās, 94
surrender (*istislām*), 49

T
tajwīd (Qur'anic recitation), 93–94, 111
takbīrat al-iḥrām, 51, 89
tal'hu, 93
talā, 93
ten wonders of prayer, 45–53
the Scripture, 72
tilāwah, 92
tolerance, 60, 65, 67–69, 119
tranquility, 7, 13, 16, 34, 132, 139

U
unity, 62, 64, 68–69
universe, 12, 16, 27, 42, 102, 107, 127, 149

W
way (*ṣirāṭ*), 117
Western civilisation, 21
worship
  acts of, 32, 48–49, 74, 86, 122
  amount of time, 84, 87
  expressions, 53, 73, 85
  forms of, 3–6, 22, 149–150
  genuine, 125
  private, 134–135, 139–140
  protocols and rules, 50, 76
  rituals, 36, 42, 51, 55, 57, 72, 80
  sound, 65–66
  use of tongue, 85
  you alone and do we, 112–115